Cover picture: Villa Boublil, rue d'Autrich. Tunis, built in 1931 by Jose G. Ellul.

Nazi Gold

Finding Rommel's Treasure

Ron Boublil

TPI Publication

Copyright © 2013 by Ron Boublil

Cover by: TPI Publisher

All rights reserved. No part of this book may be reproduced in any form by any electronic or mechanical means including photocopying, recording, or information storage and retrieval without permission in writing from the author.

ISBN-13: 978-0994029300

ISBN-10: 0994029306

cybertpi@gmail.com

TPI Publishers

Montreal, Quebec, Canada

Dedicated to those Tunisians who hid their Jewish friends, among them my father, when the Nazis came looking for them.

Printed in the USA

Contents

PREFACE 9

THE GOLD RUSH 13
   THE RESTITUTION OF MONETARY GOLD 32
   THE MAPS 38
   THE MEDITERRANEAN SEABED 45
   SCANNING THE OCEAN FLOOR AND BEYOND
   48

ROMMEL'S TREASURE? 52
   NAZI GOLD 54
   KIRNER, FLEIG AND OTHER EXPEDITIONS 58

THE POLITICS OF REPARATION 63
   GOLD AND SWISS BANKS 72
   LATE REPARATION TO TUNISIAN JEWS 74

NAZI COLONIAL WAR 82
   MADNESS OR MISCALCULATION? 105
   NAZI ANTI-JEWISH PROPAGNDA 107
   GENERAL GEORGE PATTON 117
   ERWIN ROMMEL 121
   TUNISIAN JEWS UNDER NAZI CONTROL 128

THE ISRAELI CONNECTION 146

CONCLUSION 167

Notes 169
Index 174

PREFACE

"In the chaos of those days, a potent legend was born that Rommel's men had not left empty-handed. Packed into ammunition boxes, it was said, were bars of gold, trinkets and diamonds, all the terrible fruits of their pillaging of the Jewish communities in Tunisia." (The Daily Mail, 2007)

This book is about what became known as Rommel's treasure. Though thousands of people have tried to find it, and documentaries, books and articles have been dedicated to this subject, so far none has been able to neither bring us any closer to finding the treasure nor provide a better understanding of what this treasure is. This book will lead you through the existing literature, adding to the mystery, and boldly claiming that some clues as to the whereabouts of this treasure exist within its pages.

Hopefully the reader will be able to decipher the codes of history. There are neither maps nor coordinates to lead you in a yacht to the actual location, even though I have sailed these waters many times before. I was the editor of Mediterranean Yachting magazine, based in Malta, and sea stories from the region were my business. I have interviewed hundreds of people from every corner of the world, and I have collected many stories about adventures while sailing the oceans. My favorite stories were always about the Mediterranean Sea and its shores. This is where ancient treasures from a violent past are hidden, waiting to be found. I published many of these stories, which were read by thousands around the Mediterranean, while other stories were shelved, waiting for their right moment. I have been thinking and gathering information about this treasure for years. It is now time to expose what I know, what should be known, and why this treasure matters.

The following pages were written in response to a comment made by someone, code-name Ed, in one of the many internet forums dealing with the subject of Rommel's treasure. Ed had had enough of fabricated stories, and asked: "But perhaps we are looking at this story from the wrong end? Maybe we need to find the original source of the story?" Ed was frustrated that no one was able to find the treasure. He was upset that even after hundreds of expeditions, nothing was found and we are no closer to recovering the treasure. People made connections that never existed. They built new stories on top of old ones, and many tales simply did not make any sense. So, going to the "source" was indeed a good idea. This book deals with what happened in Tunisia during WWII and who the people were whose wealth was taken – and those responsible for the looting. It will lay out the sequence of events, including various important dates, and question the different existing theories about the treasure. There were two types of looted Nazi gold: monetary looted gold and individual looted gold. Understanding the difference between the two is of paramount importance to unravelling the mysteries surrounding the treasure we all want to find. It is important because towards the end of the war the two types of looted gold overlapped with each other and could not be distinguished. Individuals, government agencies and companies turned a blind eye to the difference between the two types of gold, purposefully forgetting its origin as well its rightful owners.

Some of the information and theories in this book may be disturbing and even shocking to some people. But history has a way of tricking us all, especially when viewed from a distance.

THE GOLD RUSH

In ancient Greece everything in the sea was under the protection of Poseidon, the God of the sea. He was responsible for guarding treasures, especially gold treasure and life on and under water. The Hebrews have perfected this concept. The word Elohim means God. In Hebrew it's written as "אלהים" the most sacred word in Biblical Hebrew. If we break this into two syllables we will get "אל" and "הים", which literally means "God of the Sea," or El Hayam. These Gods were completely obsessed with gold and the morality of men towards this shining rare metal.

Around 500 BC, a series of gold coins were dedicated to Poseidon through various creatures of the sea, including the respected Seal Monk of the Mediterranean. Around this time the unfinished Temple of Poseidon was constructed in Cape Soúnio. This temple was destroyed by a Persian invasion a few decades later. Poseidon was also the God of underwater earthquakes responsible for the natural balance of planet Earth and its waters – with all the treasures it holds. Poseidon's temper was violent, and sailors and residents of coastlines trembled in the wake of his fury when storms swept the seas and shores.

With the passage of time, artistic and cultural attributes embellished Poseidon's fame. Festivals were held in his honor. His character as a sea god became prominent in art, in which he was commonly depicted with his familiar three-pronged trident and a dolphin. In Corsica, a great statue was erected in his honor, and many diving centers and vessels were named after him, for good luck. In Tunisia, an ancient (third-century AD) mosaic of Poseidon riding his horses on the water is hanging on the walls at the Sousse museum, one of few surviving items from German and other lootings. History, legends and mythology makes sailing and diving in the Mediterranean waters unique. In 1995, I received the strangest invitation from the Mayor of a Greek island: "Poseidon awaits you on his island" (Poros) to participate in a Mediterranean yachting festival, the first of its kind in Greece. No serious sailor would turn down such an invitation and dare to sail the sea again. It was here on this island that I first met with the treasure hunters of the Mediterranean. And it was also on this island that the diplomatic representatives of France and Russia met in 1828 after their victorious naval confrontation with the fleet of the Ottoman Empire...

The International Registry of Sunken Ships around the world has at the top of its list the Nazi looting of Jewish North African gold, what is known as "Rommel's treasure."

According to this registry, Rommel shipped gold, diamonds and other valuables by submarine to Corsica. In Corsica the submarine was attacked by Allied bombers and sunk, and now it lies somewhere at the bottom of the ocean. But this is only one version of the story. There are other accounts that the gold was unloaded into small vessels which were then attacked by American bombers, and six large waterproof boxes, resembling "coffins," containing 2.4 tons of gold were thrown into the ocean with the hope that they could be salvaged at a later date. An ex-Nazi named Fleig who triggered the search immediately after the war valued the loot at about 100 million dollars. Some have estimated the treasure to be worth 15 billion euros, which may or may not be an exaggeration. Considering that the whole Tunisian and Libyan Jewish communities were completely stripped of their wealth, the dollar value of the loot should indeed be very high. This young Nazi soldier was brought to the site, and once there seemed to have lost his memory regarding the exact location of the treasure. He later disappeared, never to be seen again.

For many years, hundreds of underwater expeditions searched for the treasure, and so far nothing has been found. In 1990, the French and the Germans each produced their own documentaries aired on their respective national television stations. In French, it was called "Le tresor de Rommel." Nothing revealing was said in either the French and German documentaries, and both were based mostly on Fleig's story as told by the French civil servants who interviewed him. He was an unemployed soldier, or rather an SS soldier, telling his story to French authorities who in turn had no intention of sharing the loot with him or with anybody else – Corsica was their island, and so was Tunisia. If he knew where the treasure was, he would have remained quiet and waited for better opportunities to find the gold by himself, or with the help of a private company. The French had supplementary information about Fleig's character and knew of his habits as a womanizer and heavy drinker. The added description completed the picture of Corsican bars, murder, the Italian Mafia and love affairs, as well as strange and primitive diving expeditions. Still, Rommel's treasure is considered one of the top ten unsolved mysteries of WWII. The second German soldier to appear in Peter Hanining's book The Mystery of Rommel's Gold was Walter Kirner, who claimed to know where the treasure is. This 21-year-old German SS soldier had a completely different account of where the treasure was. We will return to him later.

The gold trade was at its height at the beginning of the Second World War, and in 1940 the British moved their gold reserves to Canada. Gold bullion was delivered by ship to Halifax, from there to Quebec City, and then from there by truck and train to Ottawa. It is considered the largest movement of wealth in history. This gold was used as currency for purchasing arms from the US, and it is estimated that 28 billion dollars' worth of gold (in today's value) was shipped in a secret operation known as the "Fish Operation." When the Bank of Canada (BOC) began their massive relocation, many wondered if any of the British gold was still in Canadian vaults. Some also wondered if Nazi-looted gold was also stacked there. Rows of gold bullion were neatly stacked, as in a library, and it did not all have the same luster and spark,[1] since every country had its own way of melting and stamping its gold – and obviously every country had its own quality of gold. But not just British gold arrived in Ottawa. Belgium, the Netherlands, Norway, France and Poland also shipped out as much gold as they could. In total, some 120 billion dollars worth, or 2,586 tons, of gold was moved from Europe and into Canadian and American vaults. A few ships sunk during these operations, which lasted about three years starting in 1939. Payments for arms was one reason for these shipments, but the other, more urgent reason was the fear that this gold would fall into Nazi hands – North America's vaults seemed to be the safest place on Earth.

The Nazi regime was deeply entangled in this gold economy, as demonstrated, for example, by the Bank of International Settlements (BIS), which kept its operations in London throughout the war. The first thing Germany did after invading Czechoslovakia in 1939 was issue a transfer-of-gold request, from the BIS in England to its Reichsbank BIS account. Twenty-three metric tons of gold were transferred to Nazi hands without them firing a shot. At this level of economic control, the bankers were operating on a completely different level of morality and conduct. Their business was to ensure the uninterrupted working of the current financial system, irrespective of wars and completely removed from local politics. Only gold provided the basis for this economic reality. According to Adam LeBor, "BIS was so entwined with the Nazi economy that it helped keep the Third Reich in business."[2] Attempts failed to close the bank down after the war, and it has continued its operations to this day, becoming one of the most important pillars of today's financial world order. It only has about 140 customers who regularly meet in secret, and no one knows what goes on behind closed doors. Indeed, this strange and secretive organization provides ample fodder for conspiracy theories...

After the Great Depression, the US enacted the Gold Reserve Act in 1934, following an executive order, which outlawed the possession and trading of gold. The Reserve Act was designed to encourage individuals to hand in their gold. Heavy fines and financial incentives to control the price of gold continued and remained in effect until 1964. The US Treasury implemented these measures while foreign gold was moving in, mostly from European countries. By 1940, it is estimated that the US was holding 19,543 tons of gold (about 500 billion dollars in current value), three times the amount it held in 1933. Gold, in the aftermath of World War I, was protecting the dollar, which eventually led to a complete collapse of older economies. The government confiscated local gold, while paying high prices in US currency for imported bullion.

Alexander III of Macedon's campaign began with the gold reserves that his father had built at Mount Pangeus. They had a whole army to support their gold. The Roman Empire was similarly funded by gold mining and loot; Julius Caesar's European conquests were also based on looting treasures. The Punic Wars with Carthage were fought over Spanish and African gold, and involved Egypt's long history with the precious metal. Indeed, the Romans in particular sought African gold, which was known for its exceptionally lustrous beauty. Similarly, central to colonialism was the exploitation of natural resources, and gold was at the center of it. Gold mining and trading in Africa was the dominant factor embedded in the colonial economic structure; South Africa was leading this Gold Rush as thousands of Europeans flocked to the region, making the country a world leader in gold production. Until a decade ago, South Africa was producing about 30 percent of the world's gold. Indeed, mining – of gold and later, diamonds – has greatly determined the social and political character of the country. All other regions of the African continent were viewed by colonialists in the same manner. Up until 1930, the Gold Standard set the economic relations between countries. Currency was backed by gold and Transvaal, South Africa became the world's largest mining area in 1886, producing more gold then the whole world combined. The city of Johannesburg grew out of a small mining camp in Transvaal. The key to mining in this era was cheap labor.

The price of gold was fixed for a long time, and the only way to remain profitable was to reduce production costs. The British and Boer governments thus worked in tandem to ensure a steady flow of cheap labor. Hundreds of thousands of African blacks worked in these mines, and countless others became migrant workers, forced not just to work in mining but also pay taxes (the "hut" tax) permitting them to work. Mining gold was relatively easy at first, as much of the gold was literally lying on the ground. When the easy gold was no longer available, they had to dig deeper and deeper, hundreds of meters underground. Better mining equipment and an abundance of cheap labor made South Africa a leader in the production of this commodity. Thus, a whole economy sprang out of gold mining, eventually leading to the destruction of African kingdoms everywhere on the continent. However, it is interesting to note that South African gold production has recently gone down considerably. In 1983, South Africa was producing 68 percent of the world's gold, and by 2013 it had gone down to 6 percent. Strikes, old gold mines and no new discoveries led to this alarming decline.[3] The decline has led to "illegal" mining by tens of thousands of individuals who have flocked to the 4,500 abandoned mines in search of any remaining gold. Soon, it is possible that there will be more people involved in this dangerous gold production than in the official industry. The unemployed gold miners of South Africa have no choice but to continue to dig deeper underground with the hope of finding some sand-sized grains of the precious metal.

African gold production and trade started early in the continent's history. Sub-Saharan Africans have long traded in gold, and both Ghana and Mali played a major role in producing and moving global gold supplies. In East Africa, Sudan and Ethiopia were also participants. Arab historians have long documented these gold-trading caravans, manned primarily by the Berber populations of North Africa. In 1325, a ton of gold arrived in Egypt causing the financial markets to collapse. Sub-Saharan Africans also traded gold for salt, which for them was a much-needed and scarce commodity, although it was easy for them to find gold nuggets in river-beds after heavy rainfalls. By the fifteenth century, Europeans started sailing to the so-called Gold Coast, where Portugal, England, France, Holland and Sweden were sailing in search of gold (and slaves). It is estimated that the Akan people in Ghana alone were producing about 1-2 tons of gold a year, most of which ended up in European and Arabic hands. Ancient gold artifacts were also melted to produce gold coinage. Historians now tend to agree that gold and not slaves was the primary driving force in West Africa, for at least 500 years. The Andalusian Spanish Arab traveler Abu Ubayd Al-Bakri visited the area in the eleventh century and wrote a book describing the gold culture of these people, as well as how the gold trade functioned at that time. Ironically, the late introduction of Islam led to great divisions among tribes, which eventually led to their complete destruction.

In 1815, the American Consul General to Tunisia, Mordechai Emanuel Noah, wrote about the Jews of Tunisia. Noah was of Jewish Portuguese and Spanish decent. According to his reports, the Jews were running Tunisia's economy, especially coinage, jewelry production and trade. Preoccupation with gold was an old tradition among the Jewish population in the country, in view of the property restrictions imposed on them by Sharia law. He wrote:

"With all the apparent oppression, the Jews are the leading men; they are in Barbary the principal mechanics, they are at the head of the custom-house, they farm the revenues, the exportation of various article, and the monopoly of various merchandise, are secured to them by purchase, they control the mint and regulate the coinage of money, they keep the Bey's jewels and valuable articles, and are his treasurers, secretaries and interpreters; the little known of arts, science and medicine are confined to the Jews."

This powerful description of Tunisia's indigenous population participating in North African economy was not an exaggeration. Yet Noah was relieved of his post by the White House because his Jewish religion was an "obstacle to performing his consular functions." However, Noah argued that most diplomats in the region were Jewish and his religion was not an obstacle.

The Mint in North Africa was the institution responsible for the conversion of gold and silver into coinage, and this office was under the control of the treasurer. However, upon colonizing Tunisia, the French took hold of coinage. By 1891, all Tunisian minting was done in Paris, but continued to include Arabic inscriptions and the names of the various Sultans. All minting, beginning in 1891, was done in silver, which ended 300 years of chaotic Ottoman currency policies issuing gold, silver and bronze coins with Turkish designs. Indeed, coins found from before this time were extremely valuable. In 1990, a 20-kilogram gold coinage cache was found in Egypt, which contained mostly centuries-old Tunisian gold. The gold value of this treasure was evaluated to be $250,000, but its real value was estimated at 300 million dollars. Elsewhere in North Africa, during the sixteenth century, Egypt was recorded to be sending 600,000 gold coins a year to Istanbul as tax revenue for the Ottoman's rulers. Most of the gold was mined in the Sudan and then minted in Egypt.

A large part of the existing gold in the world before WWII was African gold accumulated over the centuries by different colonial powers. African gold from the South, West and East was being stockpiled in European vaults. Indeed, the poorest countries on earth were providing gold to the richest, and received little if anything in return – except a lasting colonial world order. In that sense, the German looting of gold and jewelry in Tunisia was not an uncommon historical occurrence, as it had been practiced by every conquering colonial power from the Romans onward. Jan Bart Gewald claims, in an article written for the Rosenberg Quarterly, that West African gold powered the global economy, which was centered on Europe and the Indian Ocean before the gold era of the new world in America and South Africa: "West African gold, dug by agriculturalists, underwrote the caliphates of North Africa, Arabia, Asia and Southern Europe following the Islamic conquest. The lure of West African gold powered the voyages of exploration emanating from the Iberian Peninsula."[4] It could even be argued that gold trading also led to the destruction of African civilizations everywhere on the continent. It was also gold that led to the introduction of slavery.

Gold trading also produced unique social and political organizations that led to unimaginable suffering both in Africa and in Europe, especially during the two world wars. After all, Africans participated in the slave trade as much as the Europeans and the Arabs. In North Africa for example, slaves were not only blacks but also whites captured at sea or in raids on the shores of Europe. One million white Europeans were captured in North African piracy; they are now referred to as the "forgotten slaves, or White Gold." North African piracy states traded in both gold and slaves, though the old world was not idle in this endeavor. By far the most serious player in the gold market in history was (and still is) India. It is the second largest buyer of gold (after China), even today. It drained the Romans of their gold 2,000 years ago. It continued to buy gold during and after WWI. In 1912, the New York Times published an alarming article on India's hunger for gold with the headline "Warning of Drain on World Supply of Gold."

More recently, the most important events in the gold trade occurred in Libya under Muammar Gadhafi. Libya was heavily invested in gold, turning black liquid into yellow metal. During his last years in power Gadhafi demanded gold (gold-backed "dinars," a single African currency made from gold) as payments for oil purchases. The situation intensified and threatened the international gold order, putting the dollar and the world's financial system at risk. The Libyan regime was sitting on 150 tons of gold in reserve, and if other countries were to follow Gadhafi's plan of using gold as payment for their resources, the western world would simply run out of gold. The situation was critical as it had the potential of bringing the Western world and its financial system to its knees, and fears that African and Arab countries would follow Gadhafi's plan were very real. However, in his old age Gadhafi moved away from Arabism and more towards Berber and African historical narratives. His rhetoric no longer resembled the Arab vision of the world, and he became increasingly alienated from the West and his old Arab allies. His downfall, however, had to do with gold. Very early in the recent uprising in Libya, analysts were scratching their heads trying to figure out why the rebels were demanding the opening of a new Central Bank. Their main demand was centered on the "Designation of the Central Bank of Benghazi as a monetary authority competent in monetary policies in Libya and an appointment of a Governor to the Central Bank of Libya, with a temporary headquarters in Benghazi."[5] The rebels, it seems, were trying to dissuade Libya from following Gadhafi's monetary gold plans.

The national thirst for gold continues today, with Iran investing heavily in gold mining to boost production from 3 to 6 tons a year. This is a major operation as it takes on average a ton of earth to extract three grams of gold. Similarly in Russia, Putin is buying gold amidst the economic crisis triggered by Ukraine's invasion and the sanctions that followed. In October 2014 alone, Russia had purchased more gold than any other nation on the planet, thus becoming the world's fifth largest bullion holder after the United States, Germany, Italy and France. Russian gold purchases were followed by large gold purchases by Kazakhstan, Kyrgyzstan and Tajikistan. Even ISIS has recently gotten into the game, claiming that they will produce their own currency based on the original Dinar coins used during the Caliphate of Uthman in 634 CE; it will include seven minted coins: two gold, three silver and two copper.

Treasure hunters have long been mesmerized by ancient African gold treasures. The story of Ali Baba captured their imagination, complicating searches for the location of treasures, its sources and its history – and obviously its rightful owners. Interestingly, AliBaba recently became the most valued company on the Stock Exchange in both the US and China, and could surpass Apple within three years. AliBaba does not produce anything tangible; it's strictly an e-commerce organization. Who could imagine that Ali Baba (and the forty thieves), which is a story of lootings and gold treasure, would become a Chinese trademark and company name, and one of the largest corporations in the world? The Ali Baba story is included in the One Thousand and One Nights, a part of The Arabian Nights. In the story, Ali Baba is the only one who knows the secret of how to access a gold treasure hidden in a cave. The thieves who had this treasure, and the other greedy individuals who tried to steal it, died in all kinds of circumstances, and Ali Baba is left with all the gold.

The reader in this entire saga overlooks completely the moral of the story that the treasure is looted gold.

It should be remembered that the Germans in WWII were not after oil in Libya. Oil exploration and drilling started in Libya only in 1951 and in Algeria in 1956. Lack of proper drilling equipment and the harsh desert conditions had prevented the Italians and the French from exploiting this natural resource. In fact, in 1940 the Italians tried drilling near Tripoli but were unsuccessful. It was the oil fields in the Balkan states, and especially Romania that were of the out most importance to Germany's war machine. The oil was imported to some 50 different refineries in Germany and from there to the various fronts. However, when Hitler decided to increase the size of his forces in North Africa, oil became crucial; he could not supply it fast enough, and the lack of fuel for tanks and other vehicles became a major factor that contributed to the complete Axis defeat in the North African theater of war. Instead, the Nazis purchased oil with looted gold, while the Allies on the other hand began targeting German refineries as early as 1940.

At the time, Germany's industrial development was still primarily based, as in England and France, on coal. But Germany on the eve of WWII was already in serious need of oil as they were consuming almost four times what they were producing, and by 1938 Germany was importing 70 percent of its oil. The oil supply was manageable during the first stages in Libya, when Rommel had only a small military force. The problem became acute, however, when Rommel's forces moved towards the Egyptian border. Oil was coming from Italy by ship to Tripoli and from there by truck, a long voyage of hundreds of kilometers in difficult terrain conditions. They had to spend a tremendous amount of fuel just to furnish basic supplies, such as water and food, for their forces. Also, Italian sea convoys carrying fuel were frequently targeted by Allied forces throughout the Tunisian campaign adding to attacks by air and land. Indeed, cutting the German oil supply was a major objective for the Allied Forces. Gasoline for their vehicles was of paramount importance, and Rommel at times had to attack English forces in order just to capture their oil reserves. Such was the case, for example, in Tobruk. Rommel was after English fuel, without which he could not have continued to fight or exist. This is why Rommel was considered at first as a gentleman warrior. Many of the confrontations between his forces and the Allies were without meaningful attainable objectives. Thus it is inconceivable that Rommel had any war plans to capture oil fields in the Middle East, nor plans to head to Palestine as a final destination, as some would argue and continue to argue even today. Rommel's forces were simply in Libya to help Mussolini guard his colony. The Germans, on the other hand, firmly believed in their ability to resolve oil shortages through the development of synthetic oil. It seems that reaching the Middle East was a far-fetched dream for the Italians, and even more so for the Germans. There is no evidence, apart from a few communiqués, that the Germans were independently heading towards the oil fields in the Middle East or to Palestine to halt the creation of the Jewish state, Israel. Hitler's orders to Rommel were geared towards holding defense lines in Libya. His war adventure along the Egyptian border resulted from a misinterpretation of the military situation, as well as a complete misunderstanding of the politics behind the military actions in the region; when Rommel finally understood this, it was too late.

During WWII, Field Marshal Erwin Rommel and Walther Rauff stripped the Tunisian and Libyan Jewish communities of their gold and wealth. Libya's economy, like Tunisia's, was run by the sizable Jewish minorities in both Tripoli and Benghazi. More than 60,000 Jews once lived in Libya, but no Jews remain there today. Nazi Germany's plan for North Africa worked, and was perfectly executed in both Tunisia and Libya; it just took longer than anticipated. The whole of North Africa today has been cleansed of its indigenous population, its Jews.

According to the National Bank of Belgium, their country's gold reserve was shipped just before Germany's invasion, to Spain, France and the US. A few ships carrying gold destined for the United States ended up in Dakar in West Africa. The convoy later moved its gold 65 kilometers inland, afraid of being attacked by French Vichy forces. The convoy kept moving inland and was ordered to return by land through Algeria on the orders of the Germans after the Franco-German armistice talks. This shipment of gold took over two years to reach Marseille, arriving in late 1942. Belgium's gold reserve at the outset of WWII amounted to 600 tons, and in 1945 Belgium demanded its gold back. Parts of it were found in a salt mine near the Thüringian town of Merkers in Germany. US troops found there a massive cache of gold, cash, jewelry, art objects and other valuable items. Also, after the war France and Belgium concluded an agreement whereby the Banque de France paid the National Bank full compensation for the transfer of gold to Germany: "All the gold that the Allies found in Germany was collected into a pool which was used by the Tripartite Commission for the Restitution of Monetary Gold to meet the claims of the countries whose assets had been plundered."[6] Obviously, Tunisia, or its Jews, was not considered as a recipient country.

Portions of France's gold were stored in Dakar, West Africa, as fierce ship battles took place between Vichy forces and the Allies. Dakar was a strategic military port, but the war was largely about capturing gold. In September 1940, the Allies sent a force of 8,000 men, an aircraft carrier, two battleships, as well as cruisers and destroyers, to convince the Vichy governor to surrender.

THE RESTITUTION OF MONETARY GOLD

When the war ended, US troops found an incredible amount of gold and other valuable items. A commission was set up to figure out who the rightful owners of the gold were, who should be compensated, and how much. The agreement "provided that all the monetary gold found in Germany by the Allied Forces, and any monetary gold recovered from third countries to which it was transferred from Germany should be pooled for distribution as restitution to claimant countries in proportion to the respective losses of gold through looting or wrongful removal to Germany."[7] The governments of the US, France and England were to receive and handle the claims. The Soviet Union renounced any claims to the looted gold. Held in custody were 10,817,021 ounces of gold, mostly in bullion bars (336,447 tons). Claims were submitted in due course by Albania, Austria, Belgium, Czechoslovakia, Greece, Italy, Luxembourg, the Netherlands, Poland and Yugoslavia. (Interestingly, Italy also had claims to this gold and was arguing for its share.) Claims filed by these countries were almost double the gold in the hands of the commission. By 1950, before the commission concluded its findings, 80 percent of the gold had been distributed, and by 1959, most of the gold was distributed. The looted gold was considered mostly as monetary gold because some of it had a paper trail, but much of the bullion found had a 1938 date stamp on them, suggesting that the Germans intended to launder the gold by forging the date of production. However, most of the gold had no definite and clear paper trail, although it was clear that it was all looted. Governments claiming this gold simply presented their claims outlining historical looting incidents of their central bank, either directly by German forces or by third-party, Nazi-collaborating governments or institutions. In 1959, the commission was left with a large amount of gold that was clearly not part of a monetary gold although much of it was "resmelted gold to conceal its origin."

The JRSO (Jewish Restitution Successor Organization) was an umbrella organization of 12 Jewish organizations from around the world. However, it never mentioned Tunisian or Libyan Jews, and their share of the Nazi loot, nor were Tunisian Jews ever considered what we call holocaust survivors.[8] Instead, the JRSO was fixated on the loss of property of European Jews. The US Holocaust Victims Redress Act 105-158, which became law in 1998, recognized the difficulty in identifying the legal owners of assets seized. It therefore provided the sum of 3 million dollars to organizations as immediate relief to survivors. The Act specifically stated that the US wants: "To facilitate efforts by the United States to seek an agreement whereby nations with claims against gold held by the Tripartite Commission for the Restitution of Monetary Gold would contribute all, or a substantial portion, of that gold to charitable organizations to assist survivors of the Holocaust."9

However, where are the Jews of Tunisia and Libya, and even Algeria, in this formula? Of course, they were not on the list; they were not counted, taken into consideration or mentioned – and no Jewish organization at the time spoke up for their interests. No government in the world represented their grievances, including the governments of Israel, France or Tunisia. The sick, old and poor Jewish Tunisians were completely abandoned, dying and heartbroken, and no one was left to claim anything. Why wasn't the looted Tunisian gold counted as part of the gold found by the Allied forces in 1945? Did they actually believe that the gold washed up on the Corsican shores? Did they believe the story told by a 21-year-old Nazi soldier who was held for two years in the Dachau concentration camp, where he had first heard the story? Tunisian gold then became a story for gold hunters of exotic findings in the Old World. The looted gold became Rommel's treasure and the story became a good mystery book, and even a Hollywood movie. But this gold was a different kind of gold, a non-traceable black gold that did not have to be counted along with the uncounted number of casualties among the Jewish and non-Jewish population of Tunisia.

The situation was so absurd that the gold collected mostly by Walther Rauff was known as

Rommel's treasure. Rauff was working for Rommel, who in turn was working for Hitler. This was the chain of command. Walther Rauff was responsible for the collection of wealth in Tunisia, and Rommel for setting the military conditions to execute the lootings. Gold looted by the Nazis ended up in the same place as all other gold, either at the Prussian Mint or Degussa, a large German industrial firm that engaged in the refinement of precious metals.[10] This suggests that gold looting by the Nazis was institutional and not an individual adventure of this or that soldier (although some individual looting did come later, towards the end of the war). Gold paid for raw materials fueling the Nazi war effort. The collection of gold from foreign lands was a key Nazi policy, the foundation on which all war efforts were built. In a similar way, looting during the colonial era was also the foundation on which the whole economic system was based in the pre- and post-Gold Standard periods. The decree shown here was drawn up by the Germans and required all Tunisian Jews to pay 20 million francs, as a fine for the

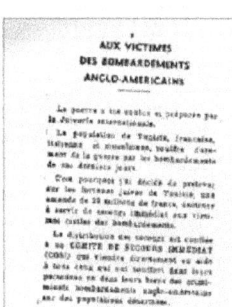

damages inflicted by Allied bombings. The Jews were specifically targeted since they were the only holders of wealth in the country. This amount in today's value would be close to half a billion dollars, and excludes the gold that was looted everywhere, either by house-to-house searches or by collective orders to hand in the community's gold. The Nazis confiscated and stripped clean every house and villa owned by Jewish families in the city of Tunis and elsewhere, making them military headquarters and clubs and other posts for officers. On December 8, 1942, at the order of Vichy government, a massive French-German collaboration scheme took place and lists of Jewish men to be arrested were compiled.

During this time, my father (who was on this list) was hidden by his Muslim Tunisian friends in their houses, and this book is dedicated to them... I don't have their names or addresses, and they probably don't know anything about this today. And even if they knew, they would no doubt be afraid to speak about it. Leaders of the community did not have a clue as to how many Jews were living in Tunisia, and they did not know how to assemble 5,000 slave workers to avoid the execution of the Jews already detained by the SS. They did not want the Germans to draw up lists of Jews to be sent to work camps, so they volunteered to draw up the lists. The leaders of this Tunisian Jewish community were so detached from the Jewish population of Tunisia that they went looking for volunteer slave laborers, and only 120 were prepared to show up at a designated place. Other committees were set up to try and have the other forces controlling the country (The French, Italians, The Bey) intervene on their behalf, but nothing worked. The meeting time had passed, and Borgel, one of the "appointed" leaders of the community went to the Kommander's headquarters, looking for Rauff. "He went to the main synagogue" they were told. On arrival, to the Grand Synagogue they witnessed the brutally of SS soldiers headed by Walther Rauff. Everyone was ordered to assemble outside, while Rauff was screaming that he considered not appearing for work an "act of sabotage against Germany," and said he would shoot the leaders of the community, including the chief rabbi. He added that he would "show them how the SS handles Jews." These kinds of stories of persecutions went on in Tunisia for more than six months, though most were done without the knowledge of the so-called leaders of the community. In Djerba alone, the Nazis looted some 50 kilograms of gold. They gave the community 24 hours to collect it or be executed. Other cities such as Nabeul, Kairouan, Sfax and Sousse also had to give their gold as ransom money.[11] The Nazis also demanded cash: 20 million francs in Tunis, 20 to 25 in Sfax. All bank deposits disappeared and were gone forever. No one ever claimed anything back, though a demand was raised that the Nazis be recognized to have been in Tunisia, and that they too suffered in the same ways as Jews everywhere in Europe – that they too were part of the Holocaust. When the war ended, thousands of Tunisian Jews left for France with two francs in their pockets and a signed document that they could not come back to Tunisia. Most left, in fact, with fewer personal items than the Nazi soldiers had when they marched to prison camps at the end of the war.

THE MAPS

In the grand scheme of the global gold trade, Tunisian Jewish gold treasure was a small and maybe insignificant portion. But it was a numbers game of accumulating whatever gold that could be collected in order to pay for Germany's war machine. The overall estimated gold loot in Tunisia and Libya was 2-3 tons of gold and silver and untold amounts of precious stones. By 1943, the Germans had become experienced in calculating how much gold a country and its citizens possessed, and what the best methods of "collecting" it were: who to send to collect it and who was to guard it. In Greece, divers are currently searching for another treasure worth 2 billion dollars looted from the Greek Jewish community by the Nazis under Max Merten, the German administrator of Thessaloniki. He loaded the treasure into a fishing boat that sunk near Peloponnese in 1943. In 1957, he was briefly arrested after pretending to be a tourist in Greece. As in the Rommel's treasure story, a Nazi soldier who was arrested with Merken after the war said he overheard discussions as to the whereabouts of this Greek Jewish treasure. As a result, a team of divers were allowed to search for the treasure in Greek territorial waters. Gold caches were reported everywhere in Europe, but only a fraction of them were found. Reaching national vaults was relatively easy and the ousted dictator of Tunisia, Ben Ali, was easily able to take 1.5 tons on his plane when fleeing the country during the Spring Revolution.

Nor did the Germans leave the gold in its place once it was collected. It had to follow the proper channels of identification, re-smelting and re-entry into the market in a new marked form in order to finance the North African and other wars. No one in North Africa requested payments in gold. There were no manufacturing of military goods in Tunisia or Libya which could contribute to their war efforts, as was the case in other occupied European countries; so the spoils of victories and colonial conquests were there for the taking. There was no fuel to be purchased and no local refineries to bribe or process. The resulting effect of this general looting of products and slave labor was a severe rationing and shortage of food items everywhere in Libya and Tunisia during the occupation. All military supplies arrived by air or sea, and locals were not paid in gold ounces for goods and services. Whoever came up with the explanation that Rommel paid with gold had no idea how modern armies and modern economies functioned, especially during WWII.

One version of the story of Rommel's treasure claimed that Hitler shipped gold to Rommel to finance his North African campaign. However, the German military in North Africa was financed mainly by taxes and by the looting of local produce and other goods. The same tactic was used in European countries under the control of the Third Reich. The soldiers in North Africa were paid in Reichsmarks. Most of them were young and could not be sustained without a monthly paycheck, paid either in North Africa or by check to be cashed later when they were back in Germany. A regular soldier was paid a salary of 12 Reichsmarks three times a month and a monthly Captain 40, the equivalent in today's currency of $51 to $136. (It is interesting to note that German soldiers in North Africa were paid considerably less than American soldiers in the same theater of war.) An allowance was also given, and officers accumulated large amounts to be cashed by their families in Germany. An account of how German soldiers spent their salaries in this conquered land will not be provided; it's too painful to discuss.

By September 1942, Messerschmitt Me 323s were being delivered for use in the Tunisian campaign, and entered service in the Mediterranean theater in November 1942. The high rate of losses among Axis naval ships had made necessary a huge airlift of equipment across the Mediterranean to keep Rommel's Afrikan Korps supplied.[12] The maximum load on 323s was 12 tons, and they were used by Germans to transport light tanks, artillery, equipment and soldiers. One of these planes was shot down while flying from Sardinia and was discovered at the bottom of the ocean, 200 feet under water off the coast of Sardinia in 2012. 213 Messerschmitt 323s were built, and this was the first to be found intact from the war.[13] Flying back from Tunisia, these planes were carrying injured soldiers and looted items – gold, art, money and even furniture. Every Jewish house was completely stripped of its contents. It's interesting to note that on April 22, 1943, a few months before the end of the war, 27 of these giant, fully-loaded planes were headed for Tunisia and intercepted by British planes over the Sicilian Straits. Twenty-one Messerschmitt Me 323s were gunned down on that day.

However, looking at the North African war maps, the Germans saw a rosy picture: an almost assured and easy victory. The whole of North Africa except Egypt was under French or Italian control. Vichy France was under control and fully co-operating, and the Italians were allies. What could possibly prevent their expansion into Egypt? A small English force on the Egyptian-Libyan border was not viewed as a threat to the German war machine, and Rommel and his military tacticians grossly miscalculated the size of the force they needed in order to win. By the time Rommel understood his mistake, it was too late to change course. Yet, Nazi presence in North Africa grew from 20,000 soldiers at the beginning to hundreds of thousands in early 1943. Retreating to Tunisia from Libya, Rommel had only 100 tanks at his disposal. He was determined to considerably increase the size of his forces in Tunisia in order to secure clear defense lines and withstand an American invasion. If Hitler had added more military might earlier, the English would not have been able to defend their colony, nor push the Germans back to their Tunisian base. It would also have been too late for the Americans to intervene via Morocco. Rommel's forces were too small to confront the Allied Forces in eastern Libya, so Rommel tried all kinds of childish maneuvers to make the English believe he had a larger military force; he had his tanks drive in circles in Benghazi so people would be impressed by their numbers, knowing that reports of this shipment of tanks would reach the English and affect their morale. He also attached empty cans to the back of vehicles so more dust would be shown if one looks from a distance. These and other tactics came from a military man in distress, underfunded and unable to either win or set clear defense lines.

Screenwriters and aspiring journalists were fascinated by the stories about Rommel's treasure, so much so that a few were actively involved in actual searches after the war. In England, for example, there was the James Bond movie writer and freelance journalist Lord Kilbracken, who spent time in Corsica talking to locals and amassing stories. What all these tales have in common was their desire to find exotic World War II stories and a tendency towards exaggeration for hungry audiences. The only people, it seemed, who did not know about Rommel's treasure were the people from whom the gold was taken. Jewish Tunisians and Libyans were in the dark about one of the world's greatest mysteries. They could not have imagined that people were searching for their gold and that it was now called "Rommel's Gold," a post-colonial name invented by Germans and English. The legal and rightful owners of this gold were a mere footnote in this story. Even French government officials in Corsica, who immediately after the war took part in the search for the gold, viewed their participation as part of a legal treasure-hunting operation. All media articles were similar, mentioning bars, cheap hotels and women in Corsica, ending with... "And they never did find Rommel's treasure."

As mentioned above, during the war, gold-looting was structural and built into the economic and government systems of both Nazi Germany and other Western countries. After the war, gold become an individual pursuit, as looting took place everywhere in the German Republic – we will return to this later. But first let's recap how much gold existed. On the eve of WWII, Germany's gold reserves increased considerably through the acquisition of Austrian gold, as well as the looting of gold from the Czech National Bank valued at $2,596,608, and later from Hungary's national bank, valued at $50,200,000. The looting continued with Albania, Holland and the USSR. After the conquest of France, $225,900,000 worth of gold was looted, part of which belonged to Belgium, who had deposited their gold in France for safekeeping. As mentioned above, the looted gold was usually resmelted and stamped "RB" (for Reichsbank) in order to disguise its origins. It was common practice, and a natural extension of Nazi politics and the German war machine. In fact, this is a main reason why Switzerland and Sweden were left as neutral territories: Germany needed a middleman for its gold-laundering activities and for the movement of gold for trading purposes. By stripping conquered countries of their gold, they were forced to eventually adopt the German currency. The Nazis were building their empire from the gold up, without which they could not have sustained their military expansion. Goods purchased in the various countries were backed by gold or barter, from tobacco and other raw materials to military hardware, as well as food. This system of exploitation was so entrenched in the Nazi economy that even as they were hurriedly pulling out of Southern Italy they took with them Italian gold valued at 100 million dollars. In short, many trading and manufacturing activities, backed by gold and neutral third-party countries, continued unhindered throughout the war. It is estimated that all the Nazi-looted gold that has been found is valued at 27 billion dollars. But billions of dollars in gold bullion, jewelry and currency are still unaccounted for, and may be connected to the disappearance of many former Nazis who ended up in South America. Pfeiffer immigrated to Argentina, Rauff to Ecuador, and their story is not much different from many other Nazi-party members who escaped immediately after the war. This was a profitable enterprise for the host and for the so-called neutral countries.

THE MEDITERRANEAN SEABED

Anyone who grew up along the shores of the Mediterranean knows that swimming, snorkeling or just walking along the beach is a treasure-hunting exercise. Your head is slightly turned downward and your toes are moving the sand around as you walk the beach. As a kid I spent years searching for treasures in the caves of the old city of Acre, the city Napoleon, the Corsican, could not conquer. I dived and later sailed every corner of the Mediterranean and the Red

Sea without ever finding anything of significant historical value. But I wrote stories of sailors who were lucky enough to find small treasures, including a Universal Cole Sun Compass found by Mr. Geinat from Jaffa Marina. Only 40 such compasses were made in South Africa in 1940. These instruments were used only by the English forces fighting Rommel in the desert of North Africa. It took us months to figure out what it was and how to use it. The Universal Sun Compass was supposed to operate inside tanks, where regular magnet compasses could not operate properly. This Cole compass proved to be too complex for desert tank battles and was replaced with a simpler design in a plastic encasing and was put to use at the end of 1943.

The Mediterranean Sea is known not just for its high salinity but also for its shifting sand phenomena. In general the seawater flow is eastward on the surface and westward below. The beaches on its shores are thus mobile landscapes. As D.W. Bennett writes: "A beach is a place where sand stops to rest for a moment before resuming its journey to somewhere else." Sand moves along the shore and from beach to sea bottom and back again, forming shorelines and barrier islands that until recently were able to repair themselves on a regular basis, producing the illusion of permanence. As Rachel Carson writes: "In every curving beach, in every grain of sand, there is a story of the earth."[14] For example, the sand on the beaches along the coast of Israel and Lebanon is derived mainly from the Nile River, through waves, storms and wave-induced currents. The building of harbors and marinas affects the natural sand movement, and serious politics is behind this as well. Israel is aware that if Gaza goes ahead with its marina development plans, fishing ports and building structures along the entire Israeli shoreline will be negatively affected. The small fishing port built there in 1994 already had negative consequences on Israel's shoreline. The Oslo accord with the Palestinians had provisions for sand erosion in Israel, and stressed the need for artificial sand nourishment and compensation.

Indeed, sand shifting has become a problem for environmentalists everywhere. Today there is a whole economy built around sand. The erosion of beaches and the misunderstanding of the natural causes behind it have led to flourishing and often illegal operations of moving sand from one area of the world to another. Dubai, for example, buys an enormous amount of sand from Australia. It is a multi-billion-dollar industry that is unchecked and often undetected, producing natural imbalances everywhere. Anyone sailing the Mediterranean Sea knows about this phenomenon. Captains of boats aboard various expeditions in 1950s stayed quiet about it because it was not in their interest to disclose these Mediterranean secrets; they were not about to endanger their source of livelihood. Bottom currents all along the shores of Tunisia, Sicilia, Sardinia and Corsica are particularly strong, especially on the eastern side of Corsica. POEM (Physical Oceanography of the Eastern Mediterranean) has revealed interesting facts about the circular motions of sands deep on the ocean floor. Corsica has become a fantastic diving destination, protected by the UNESCO World Heritage Centre, because of its natural treasures, and not because of Nazi-looted gold treasures at the bottom of the ocean.

In 2013, Tunisian gold reserves dropped from 9.7 billion dollars in 2010 to 7.3 billion dollars. This reduction is apparently due to Ben Ali and his wife who according to French reports[15] entered Tunisian National Bank and loaded a plane with one and a half tons of gold.

SCANNING THE OCEAN FLOOR AND BEYOND

According to Greek mythology, dragons were created to guard treasures, especially gold treasure lying on the ocean bed. The word 'drakon' in Greek means "the watcher." The Greeks were aware of the existence of treasures and looters of gold as far back as the beginning of written history. In Greek mythology dragons helped the gods achieve greatness, and it did not matter how fierce they were because there were always other dragons with even greater strength. Still, dragons guarded gold treasures, pretending, even for a brief period of time, to guard the pulse of civilization for the next generation. The Inka, in South America, referred to gold as the "tears of the sun," while The Odyssey refers to gold as the glory of immortals.

Odyssey Marine specializes in deep ocean explorations. It is the only company of its kind traded on the NY Stock Exchange. Almost all other treasure-hunters are amateurs in comparison. According to them, they have recovered over 15,500 silver and gold coins, as well as 45 gold bars and hundreds of gold nuggets, gold dust and jewelry, from the SS Central America shipwreck. They use sophisticated equipment and high-definition digital cameras to survey the ocean floors with advanced remote-controlled submersible robots. Odyssey's main objective is to "search the oceans of the world for treasures and artifacts once thought lost forever." Salt water does strange things to all kinds of metal, and over time most metals will decompose. However, pure gold in the salty water of the sea will retain its luster even after hundreds of years. So, considering the amount of work the company has already invested, very little gold has been found.

Extracting gold from the ocean is not a viable

option, although German scientists tried to do exactly that before the Second World War. The chemist Fritz Haber, after whom the Haber-Bosch process is partly named, was attempting to extract gold from the sea to help pay for Germany to rebuild its post-WWI economy. In theory it is possible to extract gold from the ocean, but it is not practical considering that relatively very little gold exists in the ocean, and the high energy required extracting it; the concentration of gold in world's seas is only about 0.0000000006 percent. In other words, there is between 0.1 and 2.0 mg of gold per ton in unmarked or unknown areas of the ocean. The only viable way to do this seems to create genetically engineered bacteria that are able to concentrate gold. Professor Derek Lovley at the University of Massachusetts has worked on this method, although he too was skeptical that the process could become economically viable. In any event, the National Ocean Service estimates that there is probably some 20 million tons of gold on the ocean, enough for each person on earth to have nine pounds of it. And if recent space mining projects are successful, then the sky is the limit. However, gold is rare on earth, and it is rare throughout the universe. In fact, scientists are baffled by the origin of this metal, arguing that terrestrial gold is the product of asteroid showers 200 million years ago, or due to the collision of dead stars and their explosion. The asteroid Eros, for example, is said to contain about 20 million tons of gold and similar quantities of other rare metals such as platinum and aluminum. Space explorations often have the mining of precious metals (among them gold) as one of their main objectives, which explains in part the non-cooperation among nations in this exciting frontier.

However, scanning the ocean floor on earth is an expensive operation, and Odysssey Marine as a private entity must also be profitable. They do not seem to be interested in Rommel's treasure, and the loot will probably remain at the bottom of the ocean. However, a major and potentially successful operation could be undertaken by a collective effort of French, German and Italian governments, the three countries that were directly involved in looting.

ROMMEL'S TREASURE?

In 1943, an SS unit was dispatched to Tunisia led by Walther Rauf, an already known mass-murderer and looter of Jewish life and property. Some 10,000 SS men were sent to Tunisia along with hundreds of thousands of soldiers; in order execute the long-sough-after dream of controlling North Africa.

The treasure, which is supposedly at the bottom of the Corsican shores, weighs about 3,000 kilograms and includes bullion, coins, jewelry and household and religious items. The estimated value, according to various sources, is between 20 and 100 million dollars. If we factor in that most of this gold was made out of jewelry, religious items and ancient coins, then the value of this loot would probably be much higher. In August 1952, an article was published by a correspondent of the Evening Standard in Paris stating that an American woman by the name of Ruth Bond was sailing to try and salvage Rommel's treasure. According to the article, the value of the treasure was estimated at over 200 million pounds. The crates were said to comprise "jewels and valuable pictures looted by Rommel, from rich Tunisian merchants."[16] The Chicago Tribune also published a similar story in 1952, mentioning this mystery woman who financed the whole expedition.[17] As well, The Barbados Advocate reported that Bond commissioned the Romany Maid yacht for the expedition.

There is ample evidence that the Germans were converting looted gold into bullions, which can be traded in the market place to be used as monetary currency. After all, war is above all big business. The professionals who were melting the items and turning them into bullion knew how to evaluate what was brought to them. They were aware that the locals had a totally different perspective of what gold is, its usage and its value.

In Paris, Henry Samuel wrote an article in 2007 with the title "Rommel's Sunken Gold 'Found' by British Expert," claiming that Terry Hodgkinson was on the "trail" of this treasure. Obviously, the treasure was not found, and the article was meant to keep public interest high; the media were in love with this story, both in television and print. Apparently, Terry notified the newspaper that he was confident that he knew where the treasure was, but he required new technology, equipment and money to complete the search. The paper claimed that he had "teamed up with Corsican experts and won permission from the French authorities to enter the race to find six steel cases said to contain 200 kilos of gold bullion plus other precious objects pillaged from the Jewish community in Tunisia during the war."[18]

This article in the Telegraph was one of many published over the years. In fact, interest in the story began immediately after the war, and actual dives and searches began in 1948, three years after the end of the war. Rommel's Treasure, the movie, was made in 1958, and Rommel's tank battles in Tunisia were recently made into a video game. Western media were quite obsessed with Rommel during and after the war. The English media made Rommel into one of the greatest generals in history justifying demands for more men and equipment, as the greater the enemy the greater the victory to be won, and sacrifices to be made. We will return to Rommel's unjustified hero image later on in the book. Almost every version of Rommel's treasure story is apologetic, mentioning that perhaps Rommel did not know about the looting. The looters mentioned in these articles were called Rommel's men, but the name of the treasure remains Rommel's Treasure.

NAZI GOLD

The exact value of all assets stolen by Nazi Germany remains uncertain. According to Sidney Zabludoff, a former CIA and US treasury official, only a fifth of the stolen wealth was returned to its rightful owners. He estimated the unaccounted wealth to be worth between 115 billion and 175 billion dollars. During the war, Nazi Germany continued the practice of gold-looting on a much larger scale. Germany expropriated some $550m in gold from foreign governments, including $223m from Belgium and $193m from the Netherlands.[19] These figures do not include gold and other items stolen from private citizens or companies. Much of the gold and other precious personal goods also came from those in concentration and work camps. Gold teeth, rings, earrings, religious items, personal items, and household items were all collected at a certain point in the process of extermination and enslavement. In many cases, they did not have to search for most of one's individual gold treasure or lifesavings because it was taken for granted that they would be carrying it with them; their houses were looted for bulky gold and silver items once they were gone. Their jewelry was collected on first stop on their death voyage, or at the camps. By the time they reached the concentration camps, their houses with all their belongings were already gone to local looters, or to the State Treasury.

This process was conducted all over Tunisia. The first step was to notify the Jewish population that they had to pay for the destruction the Allies were inflicting on them. They were forced to gather whatever gold they had by themselves. The Jews in Djerba had a day to get this done in order for their lives to be spared. The SS combat unit was not willing to go on house-to-house searches to find and collect the gold, except when the houses belonged to those in the upper echelons of the Jewish community.

This process has occurred many times throughout history. In Russia, it was a state-run effort but conducted by the general population. In Yemen, Jews were brought to Israel on the "magic carpet" (the name given to their mass air lift) and were told they had to hand over their gold before boarding the plane. They were told that the plane would be too heavy and would not fly with their gold, and were promised that it (and their books) would be returned to them once they were in Israel. Of course, no one has bothered to check on them since. Looting of gold and artifacts was a colonial past-time, a recreational activity for many individuals associated with colonial states and the institutions affiliated with them. In 1868, for example, the British were after Ethiopian treasure, and they sent many expeditions (comprised of colonial soldiers) where books, jewelry and archeological artifacts where stolen and have not since been recovered. According to Opoku, "The loot from Maqdala was then transported, on fifteen elephants and almost two hundred mules, to the nearby Dalanta Plain. There, on 20 and 21 April, the British military authorities held a two-day auction to raise 'prize-money' for the troops."[20] Ethiopians claimed ownership of this treasure and pled to the international community for justice for the crimes done in the past by colonial powers. In 1965, Queen Elizabeth II returned to Emperor Haile Selassie I the royal cap and seal of Tewodros II.[21] An Ethiopian treasure was found in Mussolini's personal belonging when he tried to flee in 1945. He was found with 60 kilos of gold, as well as Ethiopian crowns[22] looted during Italy's failed attempt at colonization in 1936. This treasure became known as the "treasure of Dongo." In Egypt, this looting process was out of control for many years, as ancient treasures have frequently been found everywhere, in European museums and in private hands. Many thousands of objects were taken from Egypt over the centuries, especially during the colonial period: among them mummies, statues, frescoes, figurines, monuments, tools and papyri. Some of the most commonly known objects include two 200-ton obelisks, one of which now stands in Central Park, New York, and the other in the Place de la Concorde in Paris. During the writing of this book, a group of French tourists were arrested in Paris for trying to smuggle ancient artifacts from Egypt. The French government agreed to return 239 items, including ancient gold coins, but 63 items are still under dispute. The Minister of Antiquities in Egypt, Mamdouh el-Damaty, stated in a press release that Egypt is witnessing a surge in illegal excavations and an increase in lootings from the country's many archeological sites. Obviously, not all of these illegal activities can be attributed to Westerners, as Egypt is in the midst of an unstable period with its Arab Spring "revolutions."

KIRNER, FLEIG AND OTHER EXPEDITIONS

In 1948, three years after the end of the war, when Germany was in ruins, and the rest of Europe, the Middle East and North Africa were trying to recover from the turmoil; a soldier of an SS combat unit named Peter Fleig approached French authorities with a story of gold, to be known later as Rommel's Treasure. Fleig was working for Walther Rauff, who in turn was under the command of Rommel. At the end of the war, Fleig (like Kirner) was imprisoned along with other SS men at the Dachau concentration and death camp, replacing the Jews there. Apparently, there he learned from other inmates of the hidden gold treasure.[23] Other reports claimed he was the one who threw the six crates into the sea. According to the Daily Mail, Hodgkinson, a British journalist who was said to be working on this mystery for many years, said that: "Only a few SS men knew where the treasure was, and Kirner was one of them, so his story is crucial to solving the mystery." A picture of the 20-year-old Kirner with co-ordinates on the back of it apparently detailed the exact whereabouts of the treasure. Hodgkinson was convinced that the secret was now solved and that it was only a matter of organizing a new expedition, which required more money and equipment to salvage the treasure. But this new finding was an addition to an earlier search done by Lord Kilbracken, who died in 2006, aged 85. His last expedition was held in 1963 and was based on the account recounted in 1948 by Fleig. The end of the Daily Mail article had a curious sentence about the treasure if found: "Under French law, the proceeds from the treasure would be split between the state and those who found it. But the French would also try to find any surviving relatives of those stripped of their gold." The legal issues will be dealt with later on in the book. According to the Daily Mail, German media outlet ZDF carried out secret missions to search for the gold on the coast of Corsica and came out empty-handed. The German soldier who sold the story of gold in Corsica to the French was also a 20-year-old SS soldier, and so was Kirner. Peter Haining suggested in his book that both Kirner and Fleig may really have been the same person. But does it really matter?

In 2002, an article was published in the online Divernet magazine, based on a story told by a young British soldier named Robin Leigh, who was stationed in Tobruk, Libya in 1962. He was 21 years old at the time and spent two years at an airfield base, and he went snorkel diving whenever he could. In one of these dives he apparently came across large boxes, nine meters deep at the bottom of the Mediterranean ocean. The boxes were locked and he was unable to find out what was inside. It became dark and he decided to head back to base, but planned to come back for a more serious dive. Soon after he was moved and stationed in Eden, Yemen, where he came across an article about the "The Lost Nazi Gold." According to the article, after the battle of El Alamein, the Germans decided to ship gold looted from Libya's national banks out through Tobruk to hide it from the approaching Allied Forces. There were two pictures published in the article of two Germans who were quoted as saying that they were dedicating their life to finding the lost gold. Leigh claimed that he knew them while he was stationed in Libya; they were ex-African Korps who at the end of the war became prisoners and later worked in maintenance at the Royal Air Force (RAF). Leigh immediately understood that maybe, just maybe, he had stumbled on the real lost treasure. He hoped to come back to Libya to find the location of the boxes that may or may not be part of a treasure, or maybe a part of a completely different treasure.

Diving has become synonymous with treasure-hunting. Even President Putin was recently seen diving in a shallow Mediterranean shore off the coast of Greece and came out holding an ancient Greek sculpture in his hand. It was later disclosed that the sculpture was planted there for Putin to find, part of a propaganda show of virility. In the Mediterranean Sea, as well as in the Red Sea, there are hardly any divers who are not searching for treasures. And there are no divers without stories of finding all kinds of objects. However, it is impossible that the Germans were delivering gold through Tobruk, which is 500 kilometers from Benghazi and 1,300 kilometers from Tripoli (both routes were in terrible condition). These two cities held Libya's gold, all of which was looted and shipped out during the two years of war.

To this day, people are intrigued by Nazi gold to be found as far away as Arizona, Texas, Mexico, Chile and everywhere in South America, and even in British Columbia. These tales are always surrounded by mystery, government cover-ups and unemployed journalists. Just last year, articles were published that musical scores contained the secret codes to the whereabouts of Nazi gold. Dutch filmmaker and musician Leon Giesen began a search with clues from Gottfried Federlein's "March Impromptu," and the scores were published on a crowd-funded web site so people can help with decoding it. This treasure is said to contain Hitler's personal collection of gold and diamonds.

THE POLITICS OF REPARATION

If it cannot be returned to the heirs of those from whom it was taken, perhaps it would be better left in those murky waters and the even murkier past.

–Klaus Wiegrefe

Claims to old treasures are not going away. In 2014, a painting in a Hamilton, Ontario art gallery was claimed to be Nazi loot. It took the rightful owner of the painting (Portrait of a Lady) ten years of negotiations and research until the gallery finally agreed to return it. The research was difficult because proof of the painting's history had to be found. In another case, in October 2014, 72 years after the war, jewelry was returned to heirs of its owners. The jewels were returned to a descendant of Benjamin Slager and Lena Slager-de Vries at a ceremony in the town hall of Winschoten in the north of the Netherlands. Five-hundred of the town's Jews were sent to the Westerbork concentration camp, and only 46 survived.[24]

In another example, a woman in Paris is currently suing the University of Oklahoma's museum for possessing a Nazi-looted painting. The University acknowledges the history of the painting but refuses to hand it over to its owner over "technicalities," namely that the woman's father waited too long to file a claim. The curator Emily Neff was fired and removed from the Museum by campus police under orders from administration, according to sources on campus. Some claim that the curator wanted to return the painting and was opposed, and then the University fired her for suggesting it. The case is still pending. In 2011, the Greeks were claiming compensation from Germany over looting claims. And there are many more new claims to looted artwork and jewelry. In only a few cases can ownership be traced or verified. In most, historical connections were established, but the exact owners could not be traced.

But gold was the perfect wealth laundering machine, as was discovered many centuries ago. In WWII, Swiss bankers pretended to be naïve when they claimed that much of the gold bullion belonging to the Nazi leadership was produced before the war started and therefore was not looted gold. Gold bullion was the favorite method for eliminating all traces of origins facilitating the operations of banks and governments. An immense amount of gold and personal belongings were stolen from Croatians, and a civil class-action lawsuit is pending, suing mainly the Vatican for its participation in the looting. Dr. Jonathan Levy, who is behind this important case, is determined to sue the "Vatican Bank, Franciscan order, Croatian Liberation Movement, and the Swiss National bank."[25]

Probably the most bizarre claim to the reparation of looted gold was made by an Egyptian scholar who planned to sue the Jewish people of the world for the looting of gold during the Exodus of Jews from Egypt in biblical times. According to Nabil Hilmy, Dean of the Faculty of Law at Egypt's Zagazig University,[26] the Jewish people took large quantities of Egyptian gold when they left Egypt. The amount of gold taken would be valued today in the trillions of dollars. 5,758 years ago, the Jews left Egypt in the middle of the night, on the orders of God, and took with them some 300 tons of gold, other precious metals and jewelry. Nabil and another Egyptian living in Switzerland have set up a research group to examine the feasibility of such a legal claim. Jewish lawyers were quick to respond that a counter lawsuit would follow with compensation for 400 years of slavery in Egypt. Meanwhile, the recent movie Exodus is outlawed in Egypt because of "historical inaccuracies."

These biblical stories lead us to other gold treasures at the heart of the Judeo-Christian-Muslim world, among them the ancient Ark of the Covenant, a large, gold-plated box with pure gold settings, which has sparked the imagination of many archeologists and religious adventurists for centuries. The construction of the Ark was a response to popular demands by the Hebrews for a golden calf that was constructed when Moses did not appear on time from Mount Sinai. A whole history can be connected to the Ark, from the desert to the land of Canaan and all the way to the current Israel-Palestinian problem. Recognizing that a people needed a physical object to worship, God instructed the construction of a Golden Ark. It was visible during the various Hebrew wars in ancient times until it was captured by the Philistines, who could not keep it because of different plagues which were inflicted on them in the city of Ashdod. They returned the Ark to the Hebrews, and it was moved to and from different places until it reached Jerusalem under King David, where the first Temple Mount was built to house the Ark. When the Temple was destroyed by the Babylonians, the Ark disappeared, never to be seen or mentioned again. All kinds of theories exist as to the whereabouts of this box. Ethiopian Christians have recently claimed they have the Ark hidden in Axum, and that it is guarded by a monk called "the keeper of the Ark."

Their story links Ethiopia to Israel in more ways than one. According to them, the Ark was taken by Menelik, the son of Solomon and the Queen of Sheba.

The Ark had a functional religious purpose and was shown in public for many years until it was impossible to do so for fear of looting. Their story is as verifiable as any other theory that developed over the years. However, the French documentary on Rommel's treasure goes a bit too far in suggesting that a crown belonging to Queen Sheba was among the objects stolen by Rommel while in Tobruk. The documentary mixes historical events and places, as well as confuses unverified dates. There are no mentions or documentation of this ancient object in Libya. More recent studies claimed that the Ark is buried deep in the Temple Mount below the Dome of the Rock, but excavations are permitted neither by Muslims nor by Jews. The movie Indiana Jones and the Raiders of the Lost Ark is all about finding this treasure; it focuses on gold in all its historical and mystical power and the effort to prevent it from falling into the hands of the Nazis. It is interesting to note that the Dome of the Rock was covered in 1965 by aluminum bronze alloy made in Italy. In 1993, the new renovation added 80 kilograms of gold to its dome reconstruction. Even the Baha'i religious center in Haifa has gold leafs throughout its dome. However, by the far the largest holding of religious gold is at the Vatican. The UN World Magazine estimates that the Vatican holds several billion dollars' worth of gold – most of it, apparently, is held in US vaults.

The French documentary also contains contradictory information as to the dates and the source of the treasure. It states that the young SS officer Kirner was witness to the whereabouts of the treasure. On September 7, 1943 the "Isle of Beauty" (Corsica) was in its last days of German occupation, and the Nazis were attempting to escape to northern Italy. A few days earlier, a German boat had apparently arrived from Libya with the said treasure. But no Nazi boat was travelling from Libya to Corsica in September. The Germans and Italians by this time were in prison camps in Tunisia, and the Mediterranean Sea was open to merchant ships on route to the Suez Canal. By this time most U-Boats had been destroyed. The diesel-engine U-Boats in the Mediterranean spent most of their time above water; they could not remain under water for a long periods of time and thus became easy targets for Allied planes. There were no enemies, Nazis or Italian Fascists, in Libya at that time, as all had been pushed to the Tunisian front until their defeat on May 7. These distortions or inaccuracies only led to other unsupported stories. Nevertheless, thanks to Rommel's Treasure story, Corsica is now referred to again as the island of gold (its ancient original name in Greek is Χρυσός, or chrusos, meaning "gold").

Stories of gold are as ancient as civilization itself. For thousands of years gold was used as money. Its other main uses were for jewelry, teeth and fillings. Gold is the easiest metal to work with, and has been used across all continents and in every civilization. Recently, gold was found to be a highly efficient conductor of electricity, and it is now being used heavily in the manufacture of electronics, especially for the space industry. As well, every smart phone contains about fifty cents worth of gold in its electronic components. The medical industry has also discovered some medicinal uses of gold, in both electronics and treatments. Still, 78 percent of all gold in the world is used for jewelry, from pure 24-karat (24K) gold to 12-karat (12K) alloys which contain only 50 percent gold.

Jewelry in North Africa was used differently compared to other Western countries. The old economies of North Africa had a tradition of using women's jewelry as the family banking system. From an early age women collected pieces of gold and silver jewelry, and they learned how to use it in order to purchase various items; it was also a source of emergency money. Gold and silver jewelry played a central role in all celebrations within both families and communities. Berbers living in rural areas used more silver, and their jewelry was heavy and for women only. Men hardly ever used jewelry. The urban populations of North Africa, the Jews and Arab Muslims, favored gold jewelry. It was valued by weight, not as much by the labor required to produce it. The individual obsession with gold had to do not just with its monetary value, but with its artistry and beauty, as well as its function within very ancient traditions including the very misunderstood ancient medicinal usage. Every

Jewish family, rich or poor, in North Africa had gold and silver jewelry, and household and religious items accumulated over the centuries. Furthermore, metallurgy was largely a Jewish profession in both the old world and in the new world in Europe. Already in ancient times Jews were the "smelters, blacksmiths, gold-, silver-, and coppersmiths, needle makers and armorers."[27] Sicilian Jewish goldsmiths were famous for their work in the production of religious artifacts for over 1,400 years. In 1488, in the city of Palermo alone, there were some 850 Jewish goldsmiths. In the city of Messina, most Jewish families worked as gold craftsmen.

The situation was no different in Spain up until the expulsion of the Jews in 1492. The Ottoman Empire welcomed these craftsmen and merchants, but largely for the benefit of the Empire. The most important center by far was Alexandria, Egypt, where at one point one million Jews lived and prospered. Around 323-31 B.C.E., Alexandria was the major economic and learning center in the Mediterranean. The Tanaic Rabbi Yehuda writes: "Whoever has not seen the Double Stoa of Alexandria, has not seen the glory of Israel... And they were seated there not in mixed order, but goldsmiths apart, silversmiths apart, blacksmiths apart, coppersmiths apart, and weavers apart." Libya was another region where Jews played a major role in the production of precious metal items. Libyan craftsmen were known for their metallurgical works throughout the Mediterranean, not just in the production of jewelry, but also in the manufacturing of swords and daggers, and later guns. Gold shops in Tripoli and Benghazi were already being harassed during the Italian occupation. It seems that by the time the Germans arrived, not much gold was left after it was looted by the Italians. Those who could fled with their gold and silver to Tunisia, with the hope of setting up shop there. Jewelry markets from Yemen to Morocco were populated by Jewish indigenous populations, communities that have almost disappeared entirely from every country in the Middle East and North Africa. And they have vanished without leaving a trace in most history books in Israel, as well as in the so-called Arab countries.

Wealth that had been gathered for centuries was gone in every region of North African and the Middle East, and with it thousands of years of culture. Trades, craftsmanship and knowledge were gone forever, and with it stories of gold economies of the ancient world. Somehow, the most ancient story at the heart of Jewish civilization was silenced, and no one is allowed to talk about it. Israelis are convinced that they, the Zionists, emancipated the Jews of the region, and that without them Jews would still be living in caves. Israelis are recently just starting to understand the wrongs that were done during and since WWII, but it's nearly too late to change this trend. It's too late to figure out the past, even with the help of young historians; no one seems to remember anything. No one can be bothered to document the lootings of Jewish properties in Libya, Tunisia, Algeria, Egypt and Morocco by the colonial powers, by the Nazis, or by the Fascists. In 1980s a 70-year-old man in Be'er Sheva (Israel) took on the task of drawing up a list of 700 Jewish Tunisian men who were killed in "extermination work camps" during the Nazi occupation of the country. But no one, until recently, was interested in his story. In the same way, the Tunisian story of Rommel's treasure is embodied in the inherited world we live in today. It is the story of colonialism, Nazism, Fascism, of lost cultures and civilizations, and an Islamic region of the world without its ancient indigenous population – the Jews.

GOLD AND SWISS BANKS

Gold played a vital role for both the Allied and the Axis Forces during the Second World War. Mediating between these two worlds of opposing interests were the "neutral" countries of Spain, Sweden, Turkey, and above all Switzerland. The Gold Standard days were over, but gold continued to be the basis for all economic transactions during and after the war. Gold was an ideal method for laundering money and recycling looted wealth, and the Germans utilized every avenue to both uphold the current economic system and exploit it to the fullest to their advantage using other people's wealth. Looted individual wealth was transformed into monetary wealth, used to purchase goods to feed the Nazi war machine. Multinational corporations, banks and governments cooperated to ensure the smooth transition from the gold economy during the war to the even more important gold economy in post-war era. Before and during the war, the Swiss National Bank was the largest gold distribution center in Europe; it is estimated that Nazi gold comprised the largest portion of this wealth. The bank received about 440 million dollars in gold from Nazi Germany, almost 316 million of it was looted gold.[28]

The Swiss voted to reject the boosting of gold reserves in the Swiss National Bank from 8% to 20% in a national referendum on November 30, 2014. The boosting of gold was coupled with the demand that once gold is purchased it could not be sold again, ensuring a unique financial stability based on the traditional currency. This is the first gold referendum ever taken in known history. Gold is a currency, but during the war gold was not the "currency of last resort," (Greenspan) but the only currency able to withstand the dramatic economic upheavals as it crossed state boundaries, as its origin could easily be erased. The German war machine relied on this metal to pay for badly needed raw materials; everything else was a side issue. Indeed, the

Gold Standard period was not over – it was a stronger than ever before.

The outcomes of the battles in Tunisia and Stalingrad were clear indications that Germany had lost the war and that it was really over for them. An outside observer would call the Germans to surrender to prevent further suffering and loss of millions of lives in all sides. Swiss sociologist Jean Ziegler concluded that it was "proven that the Swiss contributed significantly to the prolonging of the Second World War." Walther Funk, head of the Reichsbank explained that without the Swiss conversion of gold into hard currency, the Third Reich would have lasted "no longer than two months."

Tom Bower, argues in a long and tedious book Nazi Gold that the actions of "Swiss collaborators and profiteers" are well documented. However, he claims that the most important files and evidence have been hidden from the public or have simply disappeared. The extent of Swiss participation, as well as the amount of Nazi looted gold that went through their vaults, is to this day unknown.

LATE REPARATION TO TUNISIAN JEWS

In 2008, Israeli courts agreed that reparations should be paid to Tunisian Jews who suffered during the war. The Tel Aviv District Court reviewed the historical material on what happened to the Jews of Tunisia and reached the conclusion that Tunisian Jews living under the Nazi regime "merit equal legal standing to their European counterparts, and are eligible for reparations under the Victims of Nazi Persecution Law" (Yedioth Ahronot). For years the financial establishment in Israel refused to accept this claim because the existing laws applied only to refugees forced to flee their homeland following the Nazi occupation. Tunisian Jews kept their Tunisian citizenship throughout the war and therefore were not entitled to compensations. The courts agreed that the status of citizenship in the case of Tunisia was meaningless because Tunisia was a colony, a protectorate. It is estimated that in 2008 fewer than 20,000 Jews were eligible for a monthly stipend of roughly $300. However, in Israel the law and the application of the law are two different things. It took many more years until a small part of the Tunisian community started receiving their reparations. It is a cruel waiting game because the longer the State waits the less it has to pay out. This logic worked well with those survivors who received reparations regardless of their country of origin: only those who were directly affected and lived through the occupation were entitled. It took the government of Israel 63 years to recognize that Tunisian Jews were persecuted under the Nazis. And moreover, no one mentioned the wealth Tunisian Jews possessed at the time, and it was not mentioned once during the court proceedings.

Throughout Israel's existence, such negotiations over reparations have led to deeply rooted irreparable social and economic inequalities. This situation continues to put into question the country's moral standing. The AP contacted the Israel Ministry of Finance immediately after the court ruling stating that Tunisian Jews are eligible for compensation, and his "spokesman said he was not aware of the court ruling and had no immediate comment on the issue."[29] For years the government position was that they "did not qualify for payments from a fund set up from German reparations for Nazi victims because they weren't displaced from their homelands." Their position had nothing to do with money but with a deeply rooted misconception that the Holocaust was and is only a European Jewish tragedy, which is clearly not the case.

At the heart of the argument was whether the Nazis included North African Jews in their Wannsee Conference (during which "the Final solution" was implemented) in January 1942. The Nazis listed the number of Jews in each European country, stating France had 700,000, when in fact in 1942 it only had 300,000. To some historians, this is an indication that the Germans added France's colonies to their calculation: the Jews of Algeria, Tunisia, and Libya, which made up the missing 400,000. Historians also add Morocco to the list, but it is difficult to see how the Germans were going to reach Morocco in 1942, as they were trying to expand eastward towards Egypt. Rommel was already having serious difficulties pushing eastward, considering the small force under his command in the whole of North Africa; going west was not part of his initial plan. Scholars working on this were perplexed for years by these numbers and only recently concluded that North African Jews were indeed on the list for the "final solution." Furthermore, the total number of Jews in North Africa before the war was more than 700,000. Previously, in 1815, American Consul in Tunisia had estimated the Jewish population of North Africa to be close to a million.

In 1952, Israel signed the Reparation Agreement with West Germany, according to which the Germans were to pay Israel for the persecution and slave labor of Jews during the Nazi era. Israel was facing a serious economic crisis at the time, and reparation (according to the Labor party) was the only way out. By 1956 almost 90% of State income came from Germany. All infrastructures at the time were built using German money and equipment. Reparations were paid directly to an Israeli Purchase Delegation in Cologne whose business it was to buy local goods and services for thousands of Israeli state-owned companies, as well as some private ones. The Chancellor of West Germany at the time, Konrad Adenauer, publicly stated that German reparation was easing the way to a "spiritual settlement of infinite suffering." In 1947, a year before Israel's independence, the Polish government wanted a similar agreement with the Swiss. The Polish government argued that many of the two million Polish Jews who perished in the Holocaust had deposited their savings in Swiss banks. They were Polish citizens, and the government, therefore, was entitled to receive these funds to be used for reconstruction efforts of the motherland, Poland. For Tom Bower, author of Nazi Gold, Poland's request for reparation from Switzerland was a great historical irony.

There were 120,000-140,000 Jews living in Tunisia at the outset of the Second World War, largely comprising Tunisia's urban population. The American Consul General of Tunisia in 1815 estimated the Jewish population to be about 60,000. There are no studies done on the population growth of this group, but it seems logical, considering the high birth rate, that these numbers would have increased, not decreased.

The Tunisian Jewish population at the time can be divided into three groups: the Berbers, the Italians and the Spanish/Portuguese. The culture and heritage of the three groups, however, was predominantly Berber. Historians often confuse the ethnic question by calling them Arab Jews, which is simply historically unverifiable. Even in Israel, where the majority of these Jews live, the question was not even challenged as most intellectuals "Mizrachis" (Orientals) are trapped within a false narrative, a product of a long process of silencing in Israel and elsewhere. This false narrative, which was adopted in the whole region, is also what prevents a just and lasting peace there. The rightful owners of Rommel's treasure were not counted anywhere. Their gold (in culture and in bullion) simply never existed and can never be found. In fact, no one who can remember this wealth is alive today. There are only stories of a thriving community reduced to poverty and despair. The new generation of Israelis is not interested in finding any gold which was not part of the mainstream history of the Jewish people. Meanwhile, North African Israelis are convinced that they are the offspring of poor, uneducated and miserable parents— or at least, that's what they were taught. The new culture cannot resurrect itself, nor can it replace the old one. The new culture in Israel was unequipped to handle the complexities of its history, it was simply too late. Religion and right-wing politics on the left and right replaced this culture; at its core was a political amnesia, a silencing of the past. One Tunisian family who was interviewed for this book came to Israel in 1949 with whatever silver they still had as jewelry. Two years later the whole family of six children sold their jewelry to purchase a voyage back to Tunisia. They simply could not adjust to the terrible living conditions in Israel/Palestine. The kids were going door to door selling their bracelets, chains and rings and household items to be able to afford to board a ship back to their homeland Tunisia. They had no gold... They reached Tunisia after a long sea voyage only to discover that the country was no longer their home. Two years later, in 1953, they were back on a ship, financed by the Jewish Agency, which brought them back to Israel where they stayed. The elders were buried there in various parts of the country, and ten years later the younger generation moved to Europe and North America. Immigrants do not usually remember their past very well—especially those whose past was stolen.

The British Marxist historian Timothy Mason, a leading expert on the economic history of Nazi Germany, argued that after the 1936 economic crisis, a "primacy of politics" prevailed, as business interests were subordinated to the Nazi regime. In a 1966 essay, Mason wrote "that both the domestic and foreign policy of the National Socialist government became, from 1936 onward, increasingly independent of the influence of the economic ruling classes, and even in some essential aspects ran contrary to their collective interests," and that "it became possible for the National Socialist state to assume a fully independent role, for the 'primacy of politics' to assert itself." Mason used the following to support his thesis: "By the late 1930s, the aims of German trade policy were to use economic and political power to make the countries of Southern Europe and the Balkans dependent on Germany. The German economy would draw its raw materials from that region, and the countries in question would receive German manufactured goods in exchange." This was approaching a colonial relationship, as Yugoslavia, Hungary, Romania, Bulgaria and Greece conducted 50% of their foreign trade with Germany. German businesses were forming financial interests with the protection of the State.

Thus, the outbreak of the Second World War was caused by structural economic problems, a "flight into war" imposed by a domestic crisis. The key aspects of the crisis were, according to Mason, a shaky economic recovery threatened by a rearmament program that was overwhelming the economy, and in which the Nazi regime's nationalist bluster limited its options. In this way, Mason articulated the Primat der Innenpolitik ("primacy of domestic politics") view of World War II's origins through the concept of social imperialism. He argued that "Nazi Germany was always bent at some time upon a major war of expansion," not just in Europe but globally, including a colonial aspiration.

NAZI COLONIAL WAR

You can wipe out an entire generation, you can burn their homes to the ground, and somehow they'll still find their way back. But if you destroy their history, you destroy their achievements and it's as if they never existed.

–Art conservationist Professor Frank Stokes in the movie The Monuments Men

The history of the Holocaust has little to say about Tunisia and Tunisian Jews. Only a few hundred Tunisian Jews were taken to gas chambers by the Nazis, and only a few thousand died in the various work (slave) camps, according to the official count; no one has the real numbers in this story. The Germans did not keep records on the numbers of deaths or the level of destruction in this African country, and the Israelis never really looked at this part of Jewish history. In the greater tragedy of WWII, where tens of millions of people were killed and exterminated, Tunisia and Tunisian Jews did not matter. The magnitude of the Jewish tragedy in the Holocaust in Europe has overshadowed all other tragedies in the history of humanity. The Tunisian war was viewed as happening far away, somewhere in Africa, a place that had no effect on the big picture of world events. For decades this was the narrative accepted by historians and political scientists everywhere. Yet the big event that marked the outcome of WWII happened in Tunisia, once home to one of the most ancient Jewish populations in the world. Like everything about Tunisian Jews, their story under the Nazis has also, to a large extent, been silenced in both Israel and Tunisia. But before we examine the story of Tunisian Jews under Nazism, it is important to further set the stage of the Tunisian Campaign. This will allow us to better understand what happened to Tunisia and the Jewish community there during this destructive war. Indeed, Tunisia's delicate social fabric was destroyed completely at this time, and the country as a whole has not really recovered to this day.

The Second World War was largely about the colonial world order. At the turn of the twentieth century, an empire was measured and valued by its ability to acquire and conquer colonies in Africa, Asia and the Americas. In 1935, the leader of, the only African country never to be colonized by European powers (and which also had a large Jewish population), came to Geneva to plead with the League of Nations, as a member state, for actions against Italy's brutal invasion and attempts at colonization. Emperor Haile Selassie of the ancient and proud country of Ethiopia stood in front of the 54 member nations of the League of Nations and gave a dramatic and emotional speech, deploring the inaction of its members, crying for help to save his people from extermination and destruction. Italy's Mussolini had not forgotten the humiliation the Italian army suffered when it tried to attack and colonize Ethiopia in 1896, when Ethiopia defeated Italy and humiliated its army in a brilliant military campaign. Italy had not recovered from this defeat by a black African nation. The Italian General responsible for this fiasco was court-martialed and never commanded an army again. This time, however, Italy wanted to regain its international standing as a colonial power and aspiring empire by resuming its attempts at colonization, and Ethiopia again became the target. Selassie's main argument during this famous speech was that the role and future of the League of Nations was at stake if no action was taken to stop Italy's aggression. Leaders of the League nodded in agreement while listening to this African Emperor, but did nothing to prevent Italy's brutal attack. The inaction of the League of Nations basically ended its international role as peacekeeper and upholder of some form of international justice, post-WWI. Italy's aggression went unchallenged, signaling the deep-rooted weakness of its member states, and especially its colonial members, eventually leading to the Second World War. In essence, Europe gave Italy the green light, in "celebration" of colonialism, to invade this ancient civilization in East Africa. The main colonial powers were dividing Africa and the world among themselves, and Italy, like England and France, felt it was also entitled to colonial glory.

Germany also exercised her "God-given right" to Africa by claiming Namibia as their colony, called South West Africa, beginning in 1890s. This German colonial experience led to the almost total and complete genocide of the Herero indigenous people in 1904, the first genocide of the twentieth century. The Germans later accepted responsibility for the atrocities committed during that time, but never agreed to reparations, claiming that Germany provides enough aid to African countries through various international organizations. In 1915, this German colony was taken over by South African British forces. Hitler, like Mussolini, was dreaming of a German Empire "with Russia as his armrest; France as his footstool, England as his manufacturing nation, and the colonies as laborers to work in his Nazi vineyard."[30] Without colonies, the Germans could not profess to be an empire. When France decided to take Tunisia, it too received the blessing of other European nations. Tunisia was then under the Turkish colonial Islamic control of the Ottoman Empire, the declining and longest-lasting Empire in history.

Another of Italy's failed colonial dreams was Libya, which Italy invaded in 1910 following fierce battles against Turkish and Arab forces, as well as local Berber tribes. They later integrated Muslims into their military. Two divisions comprised of about 30,000 native Muslims fought alongside the Italians against the British army in the Egyptian offensive. In 1937, Mussolini visited Libya and declared himself the "protector of Islam," expanding the military and native participation to 100,000 soldiers. All dictators in the region since then have claimed they were the "protector of Islam," and later the protector of Palestinian rights, which has greatly marked the political situation of the region.

By far the biggest player in this era of colonialism was France, with colonial interests spanning east to west across the African continent. Economic interests and historical economic ties continue to dominate France's relations with the colonies, even after the countries' various struggles for independence. France's unique form of colonialism meant the establishment of long-lasting economic and cultural ties with their colonies, irrespective of future local politics.

On November 8, 1942, the Allies landed in North Africa, 1,000 miles away from their Tunisian target, in Morocco. A naval task force consisting of five aircraft carriers, three battleships, seven cruisers, 38 destroyers, and various support vessels was dispatched there to lead the attack against Axis Forces. Three additional attack groups, totaling some 50,000 soldiers, landed at Safi, Fedala, Mehedia-Port and Lyautey. Other landings occurred at Oran and Algiers. They met sporadic but determined French Vichy resistance, which claimed 556 American lives, as well as the lives of about 300 British and 700 Free French soldiers. This part of the invasion was largely a success, despite the difficult logistical and military terrain conditions. Within months, the total Allied Forces rose to over 400 warships, 1,000 planes, and some 120,000 men, including a battalion of US paratroopers participating in the first airborne attack in WWII. During the whole of the Tunisian campaign, tens of thousands of sorties were flown by the Allied Forces, and many thousands of bombs were dropped.

Operation Torch turned into the Tunisian Campaign, where serious major modern land and air battles took place. The biggest fight occurred in Tunisia from mid-November to January 1942, when Axis Forces had raised their military presence there to 243,000 men and 856,000 tons of supplies and equipment, arriving by sea and air, mainly from Italy. The urgency of both the Allied and the Axis Forces to take control of Tunisia was real, and both sides were determined to win this war, at all costs and as quickly as possible. By the end of the Tunisian Campaign in 1943, the Allied Forces had destroyed or neutralized nearly 800,000 German and Italian troops, and suffered casualties of 220,000 men (including during the Torch Campaign).

A series of attacks and operations took place against Rommel's German and Italian forces, involving mechanized and armored vehicles and bombers, and even hand-to-hand combat, as was the case in the battle of Kasserine in February 1943. By this time it was obvious that the German army was on the defensive as they pulled to the west after losing Tripoli. Hitler's orders at the time were to hold firm in Tunisia, promising more soldiers and supplies. He eventually gave considerable resources to his North African command, which later proved to be disastrous to his main military objectives in Europe, and especially on the Russian front.

Tunisia is strategically located on the Mediterranean Sea, and foreign powers throughout the centuries have been tempted to conquer it. The country is situated only 400 km from Sicily and a few hours by ship from Malta, which was under British control during the war. Due to the proximity, the Germans were able to quickly furnish supplies and reinforcements on short notice through its fascist ally, Italy.

The Allied naval forces were weak during the initial part of the Campaign, and Axis submarines could attack Allied ships in the waters of the Mediterranean with few Allied antisubmarine retaliations, disrupting merchant shipping routes completely. Similarly, German and Italian planes were operating during the day, and went almost unchallenged at first. At night, the Allied Forces were advancing east across the desert and the Atlas Mountains. Winter nights in Tunisia are rainy and cold, and this is when all Allied attacks happened at the beginning of the campaign. During the day, the Axis air force patrolled the air, attacking anything that moved and ensuring almost total control of the air space.

The military confrontation between the Allied and the Axis forces was not just another battle in a series of confrontations with the Germans. It was a major military campaign and to this day remains unequaled in its intensity on the African continent. Even the Yom Kippur war of 1973 between Egypt and Israel pales in intensity, number of causalities, and number of tanks, planes and navy war ships deployed. The Yom Kippur war was also the last major modern war in history where armies directly confronted one another in both traditional and modern warfare. For example, the number of Israeli and Egyptian causalities combined in the Yom Kippur war was 20,000 (2,700 Israelis), compared with some 25,000 of Americans alone in the Tunisian campaign. The total casualties in all Israeli wars since 1948 do not exceed 13,000. Total Allied casualties by May 1943 were more than 120,000 dead and tens of thousands injured. German causalities alone reached 155,000. By the end of the war, the Allied Forces had captured more than 250,000 German and Italian prisoners of war. This discrepancy is largely a function of the length of time it took for both wars to end. The Israeli-Arab war of 1973 lasted 20 days, while the Tunisian campaign lasted seven months. In both wars, however, the life of local citizens was completely disrupted, and in Tunisia it was not to recover again.

Tunisia was not under occupation during the campaign, though it was the site of a large-scale theater of war, which affected all life in the country. The whole of Tunisia from the south to the coast was engulfed in this war. All ports, airfields, roads and rails were under the control of the Axis Forces. All were used solely for the Axis military campaign purposes, and all were targeted by Allied bombers in many thousands of sorties, some accurately and others inflicting tens of thousands of casualties among the local Tunisian population, both Jews and non-Jews. The desert in the south, behind the mountains and the cities along the coast, was also a stage for massive destruction and mayhem. As shown in recently discovered archived sources, Hitler knew the importance of this war for his plan to dominate Europe, and subsequently the satellite colonies – maybe eventually Egypt and Israel; he was determined to hold Tunisia at all costs. The other determining factor was American participation in the war. Hitler could not lose to the Americans in their first direct military confrontation in history. Thus, losing Tunisia to the Allied Forces was not just a blow to his military plans but a clear early indication of the beginning of the end of the Second World War. It was a total moral defeat for Germany, and it set the tone for the atrocities in the rest of the war; it also marked the beginning of a new era in Tunisia, an era of complete and total cleansing of its Jewish population.

This war was a massive operation on a grand scale, difficult to imagine, in extremely harsh desert conditions, with armies directly facing off against one another. During the Tunisian campaign, more than 2,000 Axis aircraft were downed and 600 captured, compared with 800 Allied planes shot down. Here is an account of an air force participant, giving us a taste of the air operation in Tunisia: "The weight of daily attack during this period was heavier than any air force had ever delivered in collaboration with an attacking army. On May 6, during the final drive from Medjez el-Bab to Tunis, we flew 2,146 sorties, the great majority of which were bomber, fighter-bomber or strafing missions on a 6,000-yard front."[31] There is nowhere to hide in the desert, which made tank warfare extremely complex and difficult. The sand and mud made it even more difficult to operate these machines, adding to the existing logistical nightmare. By the end of the war Axis forces also lost some 250 war ships during the Campaign. Axis losses in the whole campaign in over a year of destruction were close to 700,000 casualties.

Underlying this "theater of Hell" was the complex logistical operation of supplying, feeding and maintaining the German and Italian armies in Tunisia. According to German records, some 200,000 tons of supplies had to be shipped each month to meet the basic requirements for the continued war against the Allied Forces, most of it oil to fuel heavy tanks and other vehicles. The Italians were struggling to find ships to bring the necessary supplies by sea. This logistical operation was tough considering the lack of large ships (especially by Italy) and the increasing lack of full control of the Mediterranean. Hundreds of war ships, submarines, attack boats and air bombings prevented the smooth transfer of supplies. The depths of the Mediterranean along the Sardinia-Tunisia route have its own hidden logbook of death, destruction and human remains. During the entire campaign, Allied bombers concentrated on the supply line, starting with ports and train stations in Italy, continuing with stubborn air attacks on ships sailing to Tunisia, and ending with its harbors.

Tunisia has never really recovered since the war. Its Jewish population was devastated. The loss of their enthusiastic support for the French, who now sided with the Germans, was a further blow to the social and moral fabric of this community. It was the beginning of the end for them as a cohesive indigenous community in the country. And, as we will see in the next section, it was also the beginning of the end of Jewish life in the entire Arab world. The Italian and Maltese populations also left Tunisia, unable to hold their historical presence in the face of the Fascist alliance and Islamic nationalism.

It was heartbreaking for the Jewish population to see the logistical and military support that Vichy officials and personnel gave to the Germans: "Vichy officials after the Torch invasion of North Africa offered to create a Légion tricolore in which French soldiers would fight with the Germans in Tunisia (November 1942)." The Germans rejected the offer. The rejection was consistent with the Nazis' reluctance to consider Vichy an ally. The French made their offer based on their calculations of how to continue to hold their colonies at all costs, even during the height of the war. Losing Tunisia to the Allied Forces, and especially to the English, was unthinkable; Tunisia was not Haiti. They were concerned not with pushing the war away from the mainland, but rather about the fear of losing their God-given gift (with the blessing of the English, Germans and Italian 60 years earlier) of their Tunisian colony. Along with Algeria, Tunisia was France's playground, its backyard.

This type of thinking continued well into the 1950s. Building (or rebuilding) empires was a fact of "political life" until after WWII. As Gregory Cooper states: "By 1955, the legitimacy of any colonial empire was very much in question, by 1965, the colonial game was over... and the nation-state was at last becoming the principal unit of political organization."[32] Nevertheless, the Germans were afraid of defections by the French forces and considered them an unreliable ally precisely because of their deep-rooted colonial interests. But it is curious that the French aligned itself with the Axis Forces, even more so than the Italians in Tunisia. Somehow, as the story goes, Italian Jews were spared the harsh treatment of the Nazis. The Fascists viewed them as instrumental in their own colonial aspirations for competing with the French in Tunisia, their last hope for a meaningful colonial heritage and presence. This was conveyed to the Germans and they agreed, at least in the first part of the Tunisian Campaign, to leave the Italian Jews alone. The Jewish community in this doubly unholy alliance found itself in an impossible situation, as both of their loyalties (Italian and French) proved to be historical mistakes for which they would later pay the ultimate price: exile and complete disappearance from the political and social maps of the world. All this had a paralyzing effect on the Jews of Tunisia. Their natural reaction of silence has lasted to this day, and in the absence of friends and supporters, their catastrophe has been of interest to no one.

The war ended with the Axis Forces collapsing like a deck of cards, and "enemy troops were surrendering in such large numbers that they clogged roads, impeding further advance." By the second week of May

1943, enemy German and Italian prisoners totaled over 275,000. Some historians (including Israelis) described all this as just another event in WWII, which misrepresents the end of the campaign. For example, as Hirschberg and his co-authors[33] write: "The evacuation of Tunisia by the Axis Forces took several weeks. They withdrew completely from Tunis on May 7 1943 and the vanguard of the British a few hours later."[34] This distorted and inaccurate historical account reduced the Tunisian Campaign into a mere incident in the history of Tunisian Jews and WWII. The magnitude of the war and its disastrous effect on the Jews of Tunisia are glossed over. This became mainstream history.

Axis Generals began surrendering on May 9, 1943, as the seven-month Tunisian Campaign entered its final days. The architect of the first "unconditional surrender" principle was a US General of Jewish faith (who enlisted in the military pretending to be a Christian) named Maurice Rose. All this happened while General Bradley turned his attention from fighting a "determined enemy to governing large numbers of civilians and prisoners." However, we never really found out what the Allied Forces did with the massive numbers of German prisoners. Pictures and videos showed them strolling at ease and in an organized fashion, each with his personal load and some even with their briefcases. These Nazi and Fascist prisoners had more personal belongings going to prison camps in the days of surrender than the Jews had when they were forced to leave Tunisia for Israel and France during their exile. Also, no one from the Axis Forces was ever charged with crimes against humanity, crimes that had nothing to do with military operations. We have seen no documents of any SS soldiers arrested for their share in the horrors they initiated and instituted during their looting, raping and killing period in Tunisia. We are also unable to find out how long were they held as prisoners, nor any detailed information on Axis policies pertaining to Jews inside the country. It seems that none of the prisoners were interrogated on this question. How were the camps maintained and supplied, considering the large numbers of prisoners? Why was no one charged with war crimes? How many Tunisian Jews were killed in this Campaign by the Axis and Allied Forces? How much gold was looted?

There are many questions, very few answers and a lot of silence from Germany, France and Israel. A typical account from a Jewish perspective is the personal manuscript of Cohen-Adria,[35] a Jewish Tunisian doctor who provides a detailed account of life in the Jewish quarter and how Jews were organized. He spends many pages talking about the cultural life of Jews in the Ghettos before the war. The Second World War was mentioned in his manuscript only once; the history of this seven-month period had been completely silenced. Other publications demonstrated a similar tendency. The old generation was both silent and silenced about the ordeal because frankly, they could not possibly explain the events that took place in their country, considering both their fragile existence and the magnitude of the war. It was for them both an extremely painful and shameful period at the same time. The silence of the new generation in Israel and elsewhere was inherited, and became a sort of a collective amnesia. They kept this tradition of silence, remembering nothing and knowing very little. At the same time, they could not possibly compete with the suffering of European Jews during the same period.

It is important to revisit this account of the Tunisian Campaign, because Israelis, Tunisians and Americans are still unaware of the full magnitude of what had happened in North Africa. Americans may have a better sense of this war because of the high rate of causalities and the existence of a cemetery commemorating its dead in the city of Tunis. But our increasingly short collective memory has eroded this as well. Even Tunisians who lived through this period did not understand the events that were taking place before their eyes. The general view of many, including North African historians, was that the Germans came and left, leaving very little mark on the Jews of Tunisia and Tunisia as a whole. Israelis who read this will understand perfectly how devastating a war can be on a country and its people. In fact, Israelis are still trying in vain to forget the Yom Kippur war.

The outcome of WWII was greatly determined by who won the Tunisian Campaign. The Germans had shipped massive amounts of military equipment and hundreds of thousands of badly needed soldiers in the Russian frontier; the best-trained soldiers were sent to Tunisia, and most were young. The Germans understood the importance of Tunisia in controlling the whole of the Mediterranean. Yet, military experts are often puzzled as to why Hitler invested so much of his military resources in this small country. To understand this better, we have to turn to the deeper history of Tunisia, which was discussed in a separate publication (Silencing the Past). It was also clear that the Germans underestimated the strength and resolve of the Americans who joined the British in the battle for Tunisia. Once they were involved, there was more at stake for the Germans. In a way, this was also a testing ground for American military capabilities confronting the Germans in the wars ahead. The Americans and everyone else understood very well that without their involvement in Tunisia the outcome of WWII would have been dramatically different, especially for Tunisian and North African Jews.

Not long before the end of the Tunisian Campaign, when it was clear that the Allies were winning the war, the famous German General Rommel left Tunisia with some of his staff and went back to Germany. He had lost a major war and everyone back home was aware of his failed performance. Rommel became a legend in both England and Germany in the early days of the Torch and Tunisian Campaigns, each for different propaganda reasons, though each acknowledging him as a brilliant military strategist. British magazines and newspapers wrote extensively on the brilliant German General they were fighting against in Tunisia and Libya. In Germany, Rommel was the General responsible for losing Africa, but most of all he is credited to losing to the Americans. He was also responsible for losing Italy, again to the Americans. Yet this same general was posted to Normandy to offset the Allied invasion and save what was left of the German Empire. He was tasked in 1944 with convincing his forces that they could fight and win an Anglo-American invasion, which is strange, as in retrospect it looks like he was sent by Hitler into a suicide mission. He could not possibly "pull a victory out of a hat," as David Irving stated in an article about Rommel. Irving, who spent 30 years writing about Hitler, also had difficulties understanding Hitler's judgment of Rommel's military capabilities during the war.

During the First World War, Tunisia was undisturbed and participated only by sending a few thousands soldiers. By the middle of the Second World War, it had become center stage, not just for military reasons but also because Tunisia had a major role to play within the Arab and Muslim world. While there, the Nazis planted the seeds of destruction, which enhanced the already high Islamic nationalist fever. In this sense

Germany has molded Tunisian nationalism. The German experience of total ethnic cleansing was replicated here almost to the last man. All this was done in a few short years after the war ended and without numerous concentration camps and excessive violence and torture, the Tunisian way. The Germans established the ground, and anti-colonialism provided the excuse for a complete and unapologetic system of ethnic cleansing. The Sultan watched, the French helped, and the rest of the world maintained its silence.

It is fair to say that the world's faith was dependent on the outcome of the Tunisian war. This was as clear to Hitler and Rommel as it was to Patton and Eisenhower. The opposing foreign armies of the Axis and Allied Forces were using the most modern and deadliest weapon systems, and implementing the most sophisticated war strategies on the battlefield. Rommel knew this already in December 1942, when he received an order from Mussolini, the nominal head of the Axis Forces in North Africa, to "resist to the utmost with all troops of the German-Italian Army." Soon after receiving this message, Rommel wrote a letter to his wife Lucy already admitting defeat, in which he states, "What is to happen now lie in God's hands." He did not have enough supplies to hold his positions in North Africa and therefore could not follow Mussolini's orders to resist. He knew that wars were not about resisting but about wining objectives. Rommel's African Korps were in a defensive mode throughout the war, holding Tunisia while inflicting as much damage to the country as they could. Rommel was consuming 400 tons of fuel daily but only receiving 152 tons, "most of which was used for withdrawals consumed by transport vehicles bringing the fuel to Rommel's mechanized units." Hitler had increased supply lines only after he learned that Rommel was planning an evacuation. He could not bear the idea of an evacuation and is reported to yell, "'I refuse to allow it. I am not going to allow it in Africa either.' Hitler then made a promise to Rommel to send him 'more arms, ammunition, and troops.'"[36]

The victory in Tunisia eliminating the Axis Forces from North Africa was a major step towards victory in the Mediterranean Theater of Operations and the rest of the war. A few years before Tunisia's independence, an American cemetery was built for fallen Allied soldiers. Bourguiba, Tunisia's President for life, wrote his famous memorial letter, and in it he complained that Tunisia is back to being a French colony and that they had not really gained ground as a result of the Allied victory. Here is an excerpt: **"Like other peoples, the Tunisian people lived through the poignant tragedy of war and through the dark hours under the occupation of the Axis troops. The victory of the Allied troops did not bring to Tunisia immediate realization of her national aspirations. It was indeed a great frustration for a people who fought on the side of freedom and made many a sacrifice during the** last two wars for the cause of peace with human justice among men, for human dignity, and recognition of the peoples' right of self-determination."

Bourguiba did not mention that Tunisia may have been under occupation, but it was Tunisian Jews who were singled out during the war, suffering great losses in life, dignity and property. He did not mention that part of its indigenous population had been abandoned by everyone, including their Islamic brothers. Tunisians lived through the "dark hours... under the occupation of the Axis troops," but it was the Jews of Tunisia alone who were completely betrayed by every segment of the population, and by every invading power. He also forgot to mention that the right for "self-determination" was directed only towards the Islamic segment of the Tunisian population. Jews were naturally excluded from this formula of future "democracy" and "self-determination." Tunisian Jews were saved from extermination by American and English forces, only to be thrown out by Islamic nationalists a few years later. Saving the Jews of Tunisia from annihilation was not a big part of this national aspiration in Tunisia. But this in fact was exactly the outcome of victory in Tunisia. Albert Memmi, in his "Portrait of the Colonialist," acknowledges that anti-colonialism in Tunisia prevented awareness of anything other than that issue. It was a disability which "prevented awareness" of other people and religions and it was contagious across North Africa.

The Allied Forces were hurt badly during the Tunisian campaign, with over 120,000 causalties English, American, Australian, South African, Canadian and others. The memorial plaque was the right place to say "thank you" to the liberating forces while honoring their dead. They saved the Jewish community in Tunisia from total extermination, and they saved Tunisia as whole from a German rule. But what was more important to "Tunisian national aspirations" then saving its indigenous population? Bourguiba played the Jewish card for years because of the large Jewish population in the country, and he continued doing so until no Jews were left! But then, it is important to remember that Bourguiba spent most of the war in either French or German-Italian jails, and he basically had no idea of its magnitude and importance, nor was he all that familiar with the complex social fabric of Tunisian society. When the war started, he was placed under arrest by the French Vichy government and transferred to German control and later to an Italian prison. In March 1943, after five years in jail, when it was clear who was winning the war, he was allowed to go back to Tunis (under pressure) to cooperate with the Axis Forces. He was jailed again by the French, only to be released in 1955, a year before the limited "independence agreement" with France. He spent so many years in jail that it is hard to imagine he really understood what was going on in Tunisia (a situation similar to the previous Muslim Brotherhood leader, who was in exile for years before returning during the Tunisian "Jasmine Revolution"). After taking power, Bourguiba jailed Islamists, communists and students, and got rid of anyone who could possibly be a threat to his one-man rule and his life-time presidency, a gift from him to the people of Tunisia, who were supposed to honor his time spent in jail. Over time, as fewer Jews remained in the country, the more ruthless he and his government became.

However, there is no information explaining what Bourguiba did in Tunisia between March and May 1943. He apparently refused to cooperate with the Axis Forces, yet he was freed from a German/Italian prison and allowed to go back to Tunisia in the midst of the war. How exactly was he persuaded to cooperate with the Germans? Was Bourguiba's cooperation a desperate act for the Axis Forces in Tunisia?

Memorial Day in 2012 was held at the American Military Cemetery in Tunisia, one of 24 around Europe. One participant noted that "one gets the impression the cemetery is a historical oddity – beautiful, but strange. The memorial, unlike those in Europe, does not commemorate a shared history, a shared sacrifice."[37] This observation is indeed sad because Americans do have a shared history in this land, especially through its indigenous Jewish population who now reside in Israel, France, Canada and the US. Tunisia also has the largest Jewish cemetery in North Africa, the Borgel cemetery, where tens of thousands of Tunisian Jews have been buried over the years. This cemetery is named after Borgel, chief rabbi of Tunis (who is on my mother's side of the family, dating back to the seventeenth century). Tunisia was not occupied in 1943; it was crushed and swallowed up by Germany. The country was consumed by a tremendously destructive war that destroyed every hope for future coexistence between Jews, Muslims, Christians and Berbers. The Jews of Tunisia understood the direction this was taking years before the invasion, when Vichy France aligned itself willingly and enthusiastically with Hitler and Mussolini under the blessing of Islamic nationalism. Indeed, one journalist with the British Forces wrote on their drive into the town of Kairouan at the end of the war that "no Arabs came to greet us, but Jews turned out in force."

MADNNESS OR MISCALCULATION?

Many researchers have recently wondered about the logic of the Tunisian campaign from the perspective of both the Axis and Allied Forces. Holding Tunisia became an impossible task for Germany, which they knew already by February 1943. Nazi Generals were aware of the impossible logistics required to sustain a fighting force, let alone win against the Allied Forces spearheaded by the Americans and the British. The Americans, on the other hand, landed 1,000 miles away from their target, moving a massive force while fighting French Vichy forces along the way, through Morocco and Algeria. The terrible terrain conditions and strict timetable made the operation risky, dangerous and some will even argue, illogical. This partly explains the high rate of causalities. It was not evident at the time that they could pull it off.

Throughout history, Tunisia has been a military target. The Romans attacked Tunisia from the sea; Hannibal attacked Rome by land, through Morocco and Spain and on through the Alps; the Arabs attacked Tunisia through Egypt and Libya; the Germans and Italians used a classic Roman invasion; and the Allied forces did so by sea, land and air, through Morocco and Algeria in the west and Libya in the east. Each invading power used its own strategic logic to win Tunisia. Nevertheless, it still remains a mystery why Hitler continued to hold Tunisia, knowing perfectly well that he was losing the war. Either they could not stop this war machine, or too many men were eager to fight in Tunisia away from the hunger crisis in Europe and from the even more terrible battles to come in their home countries. German generals were easily convinced to pack up and go to Tunisia and soldiers and officers easily gave up the fight in order to just stay alive as prisoners under the Americans. They figured that it could have been worse if they had fallen prisoners in the hands of the Russians.

It seemed that Tunisia had once again "charmed" its invaders. Tunisia had a similar effect on the PLO, which was forced out of Lebanon in 1982. It's like a soldier who shoots himself in the leg on the first day of a war, ends up in a hospital injured but still alive and out of the rest of the madness of war. Were German generals not transferring accurate, real-time war assessments to their headquarters on purpose? Were they eager to become prisoners of war? For the American generals, the Tunisian "campaign had developed nothing to cause them to reduce its manpower estimates, under which the US army is expected to total 8.2 million men."[38] The Americans and Canadians were very determined to move on with the rest of the war.

NAZI ANTI-JEWISH PROPAGNDA

During the Tunisian Campaign the Germans desperately needed local national armies to help fight their war, as was the case in Europe as well. In Tunisia they could find neither soldiers nor support personnel to help, as no trained forces existed to help a modern conquering army. They therefore had to import support staff from other occupied Eastern European countries, including Austria, all of whom were glad to join the Tunisian Korps in whatever capacity. Axis Forces were on their own, resorting to the two things they could do: get slave workers to do the dirty work as part of their "European final solution" machine and use propaganda to hopefully engage the Muslims in the war against the Allies. The success of this propaganda machine was not really evident during the war, as propaganda takes time to sink in and work its magic. The real results of German propaganda efforts during the war came later, with Tunisian Independence; the effects can even be seen during the Jasmine Revolution 69 years later. The people behind German propaganda in the Arab world had no idea how successful their campaign would become. Dictators, revolutionaries, radical Islamists and religious preachers would all use Nazi propaganda techniques, almost word for word, disseminating it on the radio and television, and later on the internet, especially Facebook and YouTube.

There are others who claim that that there were around 14 million local Muslims in the whole of the Maghreb who were serving in the North African Algerian-Moroccan-Tunisian regiment KODAT, under German command during the seven-month Tunisian occupation. In 1942, when Rommel's army was trying to advance to Egypt, the Free Arab radio—under the control of Amin al-Husaini, Mufti of Jerusalem and leader of the Palestinian Arabs—broadcasted anti-Jewish slogans (similar to what is heard in the streets of Tunisia and Egypt today). Here is a sample of a radio broadcasted at the time: "Kill the Jews who took your valuables... According to Islam it is a duty to defend your lives. This can only be fulfilled by the liquidation of the Jews. This is your best chance to get rid of this dirty race. Kill the Jews! Set their possessions on fire! Demolish their shops! Liquidate those evil helpers of British imperialism! Your only hope for rescue is to annihilate the Jews before they do this to you."[39] This occurred long before the creation of the state of Israel, and it played a role in shaping the general Arab mood in the whole of North Africa at the time. Pushing out the Jews was already part of the political agenda among Islamist nationalists long before the war. A few years later, every country in North Africa had succeeded in doing just that, and by the late 1960s, over 1.2 million Jews had been pushed out of LCA (Lands Conquered by Arabs).

The Axis Forces had invested considerable effort in recruiting foreign nationals, including Indians and prisoners of war of different nationalities, especially those serving with the British Commonwealth forces in North Africa. Both the Italians and Germans tried to capitalize on anti-British sentiments. In May 1942, the Italian army established the Ragruppamento Centri Militari, a special unit made up of individuals of different nationalities, with the objective of using them as "Intelligence gathering and sabotage operations."

Colonello di Stato consisted of a command center employing Italians from Tunisia, Palestine, Egypt, and Arabia, as well as Muslim Sudanese ex-prisoners of war. Another center included Italians from India and Persia and Indian ex-prisoners of war. In total there were 1,200 Italians, 400 Indians and 200 Arab Muslims. All received intensive army training and were dressed in Italian fascist uniforms. This experiment however, did not go so well, mainly because of loyalty issues.

The Germans attempted to do the same thing and were much more successful, especially with Muslims. Hitler did not think much of the Indian recruits and thought that the Indian unit developed was a "joke." There was Netaji Subhas Chandra Bose, a lawyer from Calcutta and ex-president of the Indian National Congress. He was a rival of Gandhi's and decided to use the existing power balance to his advantage, towards Indian Independence from the British Empire. He traveled to Russia and ended up flying to Germany in April 1942 to meet with foreign ministry officials. Not long after that, he started broadcasting propaganda to India via a powerful transmitter at Nauen. Most of the British 3rd Indian Motorized Brigade had fallen prisoner to Rommel in El Mekili, Libya. Shortly thereafter, a Lugwaffe Major was sent to interview the prisoners to recruit them. A special camp was set up for 10,000 Indian POWs in Annaburg. All were exposed to heavy indoctrination, and 6,000 were chosen to become part of the German forces; they were called the "Legion Freies Indien of the German Army," two thirds of whom were Muslim. By 1943, the Germans selected some of the Muslim recruits to be considered for the formation of a Muslim SS division.

Among the many Nazi collaborators was the Grand Mufti of Jerusalem, Hajj Amin al-Husayni, Fawzi al-Qawuqji from Syria, and Rashid 'Ali al-Kailani who was Iraq's former prime Minister. Al-Husayni was by far the most active collaborator and pushed his agenda as far as he could with Nazi policy makers, including Hitler himself. His anti-Jewish propaganda was as virulent as the Nazi philosophy of the time and was broadcast throughout the Middle East and North Africa. His messages were so horrific that listening to it makes one wonder about the origins of anti-Jewish hatred. He was financed and encouraged by the Nazis but was never fully trusted by them. The Nazis refused to provide him with any assurances as to how they saw the future of Arab Muslim countries; they obviously had a completely different future agenda in mind. Nazi Germany looked at the Arabs as an inferior people, and they had no intentions of being used by any Arab nationalists or Muslim fundamentalists. Their only meeting points were concerning questions of what to do with the Jews in Palestine, Arab lands and Europe. Nevertheless, Al-Husayni continued on, hoping to capitalize later on German successes while at the same time enjoying a monthly salary from the Nazis and a lavish lifestyle while he could. In 1942, al-Husayni and al-Kailani sent a joint letter to the foreign ministers of Germany and Italy requesting "all conceivable assistance" to the Arab world and recognition of the independence of the Arab nations and their right to unify, and a blessing for "the removal of the Jewish national homeland in Palestine." The Germans made their intentions clear by answering in a statement that "the German government was prepared to recognize the independence of Arab lands when they (the Arabs) have won this [independence]." Obviously, the Germans also dreamed of colonies in Africa and the Middle East and were not concerned with Muslims' national or colonial aspirations. The Germans did not consider instituting a new caliphate in the Arab world, far from it; they wanted to replace French and English colonial rule.

In September 1942, al-Husayani proposed the founding of another Pan-Arab center in Tunisia that would: 1) strengthen ties with Arabs in North Africa; 2) ship weapons, agents, equipment, and money to stiffen Muslim resistance in the event of an Allied landing; and 3) recruit and train Arab soldiers, who would stand prepared to defend North Africa "against any threat from the Allies, Bolshevism, and Judaism." When the Allies landed in North Africa, he made this proposal again, but apparently Hitler "wanted nothing from the Arabs." Nevertheless, Tunisia "enjoyed" around-the-clock radio hate programs from German transmitters in Greece and Italy. Al-Husayani was basically indoctrinating a new generation of Muslims, teaching them about the Jewish conspiracy and the "correct" view of the Jews in the Holy Koran, most of it borrowed from Nazi hate speech. People in North Africa listened to this kind of propaganda during the Second World War, and continue listening to the same kind of propaganda today. Nothing much has changed in this respect, only the voices and the technology, the superior transmitters and types of media. His favorite line was that the Jews were the enemies of Islam, and he did his utmost to convince his listeners of that. In one speech given in December 1942 at the newly constructed Islamic center in Berlin (Islamische Zentral-Institut), he said that the Koran judged the Jews "to be the most irreconcilable enemies of the Muslims." His speech was well covered by the mainstream Nazi media in Germany and was broadcasted to the rest of the Arab world, including Tunisia.

Despite the Allied victory in Tunisia, Nazism left the country with the long-lasting presence of Western-style anti-Semitism, which has been exploited to the fullest by Islamic interests, both moderate and radical, and by the fact that the Koran can provide plenty of room for such interpretation, as in every other Holy Book. Jeffrey Herf has gone into detail on the magnitude and the effects of these propaganda activities.[40] His thesis stipulates that there existed a "continuity and lineages between Nazism's Arabic language propaganda on the one hand and radical Islam in the subsequent decades, on the other." European hatred of Jews received a new life in the Arab world with plenty of support from their own religious beliefs and historical backgrounds. Most of the anti-Jewish rhetoric of hate was previously unknown in the Muslim world, especially in Tunisia under the Ottoman Empire. Thousands of broadcasting hours and millions of leaflets were thrown from planes into every country in North Africa and the Middle East during a period of four years. Curiously, Edward Said wrote that he decided to exclude Germany from his "Orientalism" theory because Germany was not "an imperial power and had no national interest in the Orient." He thus missed an important and crucial link to understanding events in the Arab world, helping little to aid our understanding of the current Arab Spring Revolutions or the Palestinian-Israeli conflict.

The official story of Bourguiba's stand during the Tunisian Campaign was that the Nazis attempted to pressure him into helping the "Axis powers with his influence over the Tunisian independence fighters in pushing back the Allied invasion of North Africa. Bourguiba refused and was released from prison in 1943"[41] to come back to Tunisia two months before the end of the war and after five years of French, German and Italian prisons. Bourguiba was apparently walking the fine line between his belief that the Allied Forces would win the war and his quest for Tunisian Muslim Independence. The Germans and Italians were fighting one of the major wars in WWII and it is inconceivable that they would let Bourguiba roam the streets of Tunisia free and in opposition to their own cause in this vicious and crucial war. But the Germans did not need Bourguiba's help in this war. The Axis Forces had over a half-million trained soldiers and support personnel; they needed fuel, food, ammunition and Jewish slaves. What could Bourguiba possibly have to offer? Tunisian independence fighters were basically nonexistent and mattered little in this war. The German propaganda machine was designed to divide and rule through hate laying out conditions for easy loot.

In this sense Bourguiba was a pawn, used like everyone else in Tunisia at the time. There was no need for his support, but his support would not be rejected by the Nazis if offered. His refusal to cooperate with Axis Forces is the accepted narrative in every publication, though none of them goes into detail as to why he was released from German and Italian prisons, or how they tried to convince him to cooperate. In March 1943, he made a noncommittal broadcast which was enough apparently for the Italians to let him go back to Tunisia, as there were many other New Destour party members who could not but admire and support the German's military might and occupation. At the end of the war the French accused him of collaboration with the Nazis and he had to flee again, this time to Egypt, to escape imprisonment. He spent so many years in jail and in exile that the whole of Tunisia including the Jews felt indebted to him. He, in return accepted with humility their offer, promising to remain their president for life and above all promising that the final solution to the Jews of Tunisia would be implemented as peacefully and quickly and as humanly as possible.

Much has been written about the relationship between Hooker Doolittle, the American Council General in Tunisia, and the young Bourguiba, who later named a street after him. They first met immediately after the war in 1943 when Bourguiba was trying to earn American support for his nationalist movement and secure his freedom again after the French took back control of their protectorate. Doolittle sympathized with Bourguiba's nationalist aspirations, a stand which later led to his removal and reassignment to Morocco. The official American policy was not to interfere with the balance of power in the country, and he was instructed in 1942 to change course and halt involvement in any local activities. Here is the official American view at that time: "The state Department would consider any attempt to turn the Arab population against the French as dangerous to the highest degree. Our policy is directed to building up the confidence of the French authorities and the French population in general, and induces them to support the democratic cause... While the feelings of the Arab population are of some concern to us, the French position is of much greater importance. If we were implicated in a political overturn such as you suggest, it might arouse such bitter resentment on the part of the French that we might presently find ourselves ejected from North Africa altogether."[42]

It is evident that the Americans were preparing for war and wanted no surprises from unknown local populations as to their war plans and intentions. It is also evident that the local population was strategically important to neither the Germans nor the Americans. Doolittle had no information on Allied war plans and he therefore tried on his own to mingle with local politics against Vichy control in Tunisia. A week after the American landing he left Tunisia for Algeria to return six months later. In any event, no written communication from him exists on the Jewish question in Tunisia because frankly, there was no such a thing as a Jewish question. The Americans were dead-set on winning the war; the French were preoccupied with keeping their protectorate no matter what; and the nationalists had their own vision of Tunisia stripped of its Jews.

GENERAL GEORGE PATTON

Few generals in history have left such a decisive historical mark on the outcome of wars. Patton is one of those men. The Allied Forces were in a problematic situation during the first two months of the Tunisian campaign, as casualties were extremely high. The Germans were better organized, had a better war machine and almost total air superiority. The Allies were not properly coordinated, and American infantry and mechanized armored divisions were not sufficiently trained. One German officer interviewed for a documentary said that they were amazed at the low level of military strategy the Allies had demonstrated. They were "fighting like children," he said about the early part of the Tunisian Campaign. The English were controlling the campaign, trying to guard their colonies at all costs, and the French did not really participate alongside the Allied Forces for fear of losing control of their Tunisian colony. The Free French Army later joined the Allied Forces with some 10,000 men. The Allies also made every conceivable error, underestimating the enemy's military and strategic capabilities.

Patton began his European campaign in Tunisia knowing well from reading his maps and history books that control of the country meant control of the heart of the Mediterranean, and consequently, free access from Europe to Asia and Africa. Patton's notes, letters and communiqués suggested that he understood the history of war in Tunisia, and the Hollywood movie Patton was on the mark in making a historical reference to an earlier Tunisian war, 2,000 years previous. His knowledge of the military history of the region proved to be invaluable in entering this theater of war, and winning. Training his forces for combat in a short time proved to be his main task, without which the number of casualties would have been much greater. In this sense, Tunisia became a training ground for American and Allied Forces for the wars ahead.

Patton's military drive and strategies were legend in World War II. His ruthless approach was part of his strategy, though his political views were a whole different story, and he made no secret of them. He was a soldier and a General with a focused objective of winning the war – nothing else really mattered. He built his own image, which served his purpose of securing a victory. He obviously knew that having an image of a great warrior affected not only the morale of his men but also the morale of the enemy. And indeed, from recently released German archives we know that his image preceded him. He was feared by the Germans and Italians, and was respected by his troops. The English painted Rommel as the most brilliant and fearless German general, while the Germans had Patton to worry about, painting him as the greatest General of all time.

Jeffrey Bernard, in an article "Patton Tank Mark," suggests a long recovery for Patton's training efforts, and claims that according to the Army Researchers, it will take 1,000 years for the ecology of the California's Mojave Desert to recover as a result of the intense training Patton instituted in the 1940s in preparation for WWII.[43] Imagine what the numerous tank battles have done to Tunisia's ecology.

The web is full of conspiracy theories revolving around his death by car accident in 1945. Many Jewish writers pointed to his anti-Semitic remarks concerning the DPs (Displaced Prisoners) who were scattered in camps after the war. At one point Patton writes, "I cannot understand who had the presumption to attribute to me anti-Semitic ideas which I certainly do not possess." He had been accused of making anti-Semitic remarks towards the Jews and of caring for German well-being more than those of the DPs after the war. Patton was preoccupied with the madness of war, and human and social values were according to him related to man's ability to wage war. His problem was mostly attributed to the unbearable sight of displaced people who were incapable of fighting. After experiencing so many battles and so much death, he had little respect and even less understanding for those who did not fight, irrespective of their situation.

On April 8, 1945, Patton learned that what his soldiers found at Merkers mine was not just cash and artwork, but also a large quantity of gold. The gold aspect of the find made him declare that it is now a political question, and that the whole rescue operation should be handed over to the Supreme Headquarters, commanded by Gen. Dwight D. Eisenhower.[44] The German official who was with the Generals when they entered the mine said to them this was the "last gold reserve in Germany, badly needed to pay the German army." Patton would later write that he saw "a number of suitcases filled with jewelry, such as silver and gold cigarette cases, wristwatch cases, spoons, forks, vases, gold-filled teeth, false teeth, etc." Most were smashed, ready to be converted into gold bullion and silver. The movie Brass Target, based on the novel The Algonquin Project, developed the idea that Patton's death was not an accident, but a conspiracy to steal the looted gold.

MARSHAL ERWIN ROMMEL

The more we search, the more complex the story becomes. It involves multiple countries across different continents. Hundreds of publications, at times conflicting with one another, have been published over the years about the North African theater in WWII. It's hard to imagine people agreeing on anything when it comes to the Second World War. Europe and the New World were heavily involved not only in the actual fighting but also in how the geopolitical situation was later interpreted. Rommel's participation in the North African war is controversial, but since the treasure is named after him we must deal with some of the controversies.

Rommel's son, Manfred, became the mayor of Stuttgart for 20 years. He was a respectable German citizen from the same region where he grew up with his father. He told the story of his father committing an "honorable" forced suicide, on October 14, 1944. At the age of 15, Manfred was already a soldier and was stationed in an air defense unit not far from where he lived. He came home for a two-day leave only to find his father in a life-threatening situation when an SS unit was dispatched to his house. His father told him that he would either be promoted again to the Eastern front or be tried for treason. He did not know until the last minute why the SS were outside his door. His father went out to speak with them and came back inside, telling his son that he was given a choice of death either by swallowing a poison pill, terminating his life and receiving an honorable name for him and his family, or end his life in prison for treason. Manfred said that his father had ten minutes to say good-bye. Just before exiting, Rommel turned to his son, pulled out his wallet and said that he had 150 Deutschmarks (less than $50) in it and wanted his son to have it. His assistant said to him that "this is not important" and Rommel "slowly put back the wallet in his vest" and walked to the waiting SS vehicle. This was part of what Manfred told everyone to emphasize that his father had no money or gold hidden anywhere. It is difficult to imagine that anyone, a few minutes before their death, would think about a few Deutschmarks in their pocket. This was indeed a strange story, as told by his son. In any event, twenty minutes later Rommel's family received a call that Field Marshal Rommel had died of unknown causes. He received a full state funeral as a legendary military man who sacrificed his life for the fatherland.

Much Rommel hero-worship sprang up all over. He had become an honorable military man, a soldier not a murderer, with a long trail of destruction from Egypt to Tunisia. In one documentary, a British soldier who was interviewed claimed that Rommel and his African Korps brought "great honor to Germany." Samuel Bradshaw, a 2nd lieutenant in the British 8th division, said that he and his comrades had great respect for Rommel and his troops.[45] In 1970, the German navy named a destroyer after him.

This quote, taken from Secrets of the World's Undiscovered Treasures, by Lionel and Patricia Fanthorp, was typical of an accepted interpretation and perception of Rommel's military activities in North

Africa: "Rommel, known as the Desert Fox because of his daring and cunning military tactics, was in charge of Hitler's forces in North Africa during the Second World War. During the period when he was most successful, Rommel knew that foreign currencies such as German deutschmarks were not particularly acceptable in North Africa. Instead he used gold, silver and diamonds, which were universally welcomed in wartime. Being able to buy what he needed when he needed it was one of the factors that enabled Rommel to carry out Hitler's wishes."

This view was adapted by many, including the many shipwreck hunters for lost gold. One of these groups even suggested that Rommel was paid by Hitler in gold and diamonds while in North Africa. However, all research suggests that this is completely false. The image of a heroic Desert Fox that he earned was built by the English in order to justify and glorify their own war efforts. Even Wikipedia currently has him as "one of the most skilled commanders of desert warfare in the conflict." The second part of the quote is also unfounded, as Rommel's forces did not pay gold for local services; there is no evidence suggesting this. Gold had only one direction, towards Germany's vaults as payment for raw materials, fuel and military equipment. In Tunisia, Rommel was using French currencies looted from fines levied on the Jewish population. The Messerschmitt Me 323 Gigant planes that landed in Tunisia did not fly back empty. The gold that was looted from them was on board every Messerschmitt that flew back. It is recorded by Jews in Tunis that even looted furniture was on board these planes. Until early 1943, Axis Forces controlled the air space and had no problem flying these giant planes. The transfer of gold from Tunisia to Germany was urgent, the basis for all of Rommel's military activities in both Tunisia and Libya. The Axis Forces in North Africa continued to receive their payrolls standing in line waiting for their turn to get paid. And, they were paid in Deutschmarks, not in gold.

We have to pay attention to the dates of these historical events because the above publication erroneously writes that "Rommel was forced to retreat first to Tunisia and then to Sicily." Indeed, Rommel left North Africa, but not by retreating; instead, he was called back to Germany. His orders for North Africa were to collect and ship as much gold as possible. Nothing else mattered. On March 9, 1943, two months before the end of the Tunisian Campaign, Rommel headed back by plane to Germany in order to report on the serious situation in Tunisia. Interestingly, he left Tunisia a day after General Patton received command of the II Corps, following the disastrous Battle of Kasserine Pass. Recent archive documents reveal that the Germans feared this American General. Rommel kept losing every front he commanded. He kept fleeing the battlefield in each important confrontation, either for personal health reasons, vacation or to see his wife, Lucy. General Hans-

Jürgen von Arnim replaced Rommel as the Field Marshal of the Afrikan Korps based in Tunisia. Von Arnim, who was fighting a losing battle, was captured on May 12, 1943 and became a prisoner of war at Camp Clinton, Mississippi. Hundreds of thousands prisoners in Tunisia were taken by the Allied Forces and many were shipped to Texas, where they interacted with the local American population, visiting towns without guards: "Black American guards noted that German Nazis prisoners could visit segregated restaurants that they could not."[46] In 1947 General Hans-Jürgen von Arnim returned to Germany. He died in 1962.

Rommel did not stick around to see how everything crumbled. He already knew the outcome at the beginning of 1943. He convinced Hitler that he needed more troops and equipment, and within a short time he dramatically increased his forces. I have argued elsewhere that soldiers and generals knew early on that they were about to lose the war, despite the new equipment and increased manpower. Most of them preferred life as prisoners than participating in the continuation of even bloodier wars and food shortages in European lands. The sun and beaches of Tunisia had worked their magic again. Hitler had poured in his best soldiers and the best military equipment in Tunisia. His whole military campaign in Europe depended on the outcome in North Africa. I would not be surprised to learn that Rommel's death by poison was not due to his participation in a Hitler assassination plot, but rather because of his failures to deliver victory – which is paramount to treason, or even worse. For Hitler, Rommel was a brilliant military man, who by the end lost every war on every front. Suicide was the only honorable thing Rommel could have performed in service of the Third Reich.

Rommel left behind him a trail of destruction from Egypt to Tunisia. El Alamein today has more tombs then local inhabitants. The population of the town is 7,000 people. Its German memorial has 4,200 names and Italian memorial 5,200. The Greeks have their own cemetery, and the Commonwealth its own memorial with the names of hundreds of Canadians. Tripoli was his last stop in his retreat to Tunisia. The Jews of Tripoli and Benghazi, as in Tunis, were merchants and jewelers, and were the main urban population of the cities. Some 40,000 Jews lived in the city of Tripoli and about 20,000 in Benghazi. On February 12, 1941 Rommel, on the request of the Italians, arrived in Libya. The African Korps were created to help Italy with its colonial holds of expansion in Africa. A month earlier Hitler stated that Germany must come to Italy's rescue for "political, psychological and strategic reasons," knowing perfectly well that there were other German interests on the agenda. What he did not know was that it was an impossible task. The English were inflicting heavy causalities on the Italians who were trying to advance to Egypt. By 1941 Italy was losing the battle trying to expand and some 150,000 soldiers were captured as prisoners of war and tens of thousands dead. Rommel's initial objective to help secure Libya turned into a whole campaign to control the whole of North Africa. Rommel's kept losing grip of the situation and could not rely nor lead the Italian forces he was supposed to help. He continued his trail of destruction with the construction of the Atlantic Wall in Normandy. 300,000 forced slave laborers worked to build a massive wall and defense lines construction that would last a thousand years. Thousands died in the process. These lines survived only one day, despite Rommel's abundant money and gold used to withstand the Allied attack.

TUNISIAN JEWS UNDER NAZI CONTROL

The Jewish people of Tunisia were not an ethnic group in Tunisia, nor were they a small community on the margins of Tunisian society, which was how they were portrayed in Israel; in Tunisia, they were totally forgotten. The Jews, who mostly lived in urban centers, were **Tunisia**. They were the forgotten holocaust survivors who lost not just their property but also their country. For centuries they were inseparable from the rest of the Tunisian population. Events beyond their control revealed their precarious situation during WWII, which I have sketched above: The French colonialists proved to be unreliable, after Vichy's new alliance with the Germans which began in 1940; Arab Tunisian nationalists, mixed with radical Islamists, had no interest in having Jews amongst them and behaved accordingly; the German occupation lasted for seven months, from November 1942 to May 1943, and featured a massive military campaign between the Allied and Axis Forces.

As we have seen, the Tunisian war campaign was not just another battle in WWII. Massive forces were directly confronting one another, using the best equipment available in modern warfare, and each side was completely determined to win a victory of territory and morale that would also ultimately decide the outcome of WWII. The Axis Forces in Tunisia had about half a million soldiers, tons of equipment coming through all ports every day, and airfields flooded with Axis bombers. All this was happening in a country of two million people, where only 15–20% lived in urban centers, a large percentage of whom were Jewish Tunisians. The Germans were desperate for supplies, especially food items. They were also in need of local manpower to help maintain their military holds. This was a major problem throughout the long-lasting war. The Allied Forces did not know at the time that Axis Forces were not receiving the necessary military and basic supplies. They also did not know the magnitude of the low morale of German forces once they had retreated back to Tunisia from Libya. By January 1943, the Germans understood that they had to rely on locals for foodstuffs and other basic needs, including manual slave labor to maintain their military camps. It was also obvious from the behavior of POWs that most would have loved to just bask in the Tunisian sun and sand. This huge army needed local support to sustain itself. The Germans who looted local food supplies suddenly noticed that produce and other food items were being shipped out of Tunis in carriages, and that dollar bills were circulating in the markets. The Germans caught an American soldier who was smuggled in one of these carriages and whose mission was to purchase produce for the Allied Forces, who were also desperately in need of food – and prepared to pay handsomely for it. The locals were squeezed thin and could not have survived much longer. It can be argued that these demands for supplies alone resulted in the complete destruction of Tunisian economy and social order.

The Jews were the ones singled out to do the dirty work. The Germans could not ask the Muslim population for fear of alienating them, so they naturally turned to the Jews, Tunisia's urban inhabitants. It did not take long for them to build some 30 work camps around the various military bases in the country. All Jews were forced to wear the yellow Star of David, except some Jewish-Italian elites. The Jews resisted, as they had not forgotten that for centuries they had been forced to wear similar symbols distinguishing themselves from the rest of the population under various Islamic regimes. Indeed, in Tunisia, the yellow-star identification for Jews was not a German invention. The original plan of extermination was drawn in 1942 by SS Special Forces and led by Lieutenant Colonel Walther Rauff, who as we know was already an experienced mass murderer responsible for the construction and implementation of mobile extermination gas units. A 1977 article by Der Spiegel stated that Rauff and his men were empowered to "take executive measures against the civilian population," Nazi jargon for looting, robbery, murder, rape and enslavement. The original plan was to continue to Palestine after securing Libya and Egypt. The following chapter deals with the shocking story of Walther Rauff, the treasure and the surprise and unthinkable connections.

German forces were stopped by the English and retreated first to Libya and subsequently to their original Tunisian African base: "The Desert Fox campaign led by the English was in fact a major blow to Rommel's invincibility." According to Jan Freedman, the Germans had a whole network of labor camps throughout Tunisia and during the German occupation, and at least 2,500 Jews died in them. Thousands of others were forced to work in extremely harsh conditions. According to

Freedman, the regular army was also involved in these executions. On the island of Djerba alone, Rauff's men forced the seizure of silver, gold, jewelry and other sacred items from the Jewish population. Apparently, the SS later disposed of "Rommel's Treasure" in the sea, attracting generations of treasure hunters; however, as is well known, it has never been found. Treasure hunters these days are also very busy trying to find the 13 billion dollars in gold bullion and cash hidden by Ben Ali and his wife Leila (president of the Arab Women's Organization) over a twenty-year period of corruption, deceit and looting of Tunisian and Jewish properties. This treasure has also never been found.

Little research or analysis has been undertaken on the history of Tunisian Jews during WWII, and only during the past decade has anyone started to take notice of this situation. Information is now sketchy, as few are alive to tell their story. Since 1977, some Tunisian Jewish survivors have been meeting every year on December 9 in France to remember the Nazis and hear personal accounts. It was natural that the Tunisian Council General was absent from this event since the Spring Revolution began. But stories have emerged of how Rauff and his SS forces entered the synagogue on Paris Avenue in the middle of a prayer, shooting and destroying everything in sight, exactly as they did in Paris in July 1942, as well as in Warsaw. Gilbert Habib, Gilbert Taieb, Georges Smadja, Charles Zeitoun and a few others were there every year to tell their personal stories. But the rest remained silent for decades in Israel, which in turn was not interested in documenting this story. Next year, there may be no one around to recount anything.

For years, only a handful of Tunisians wanted to speak about this period, and even fewer people wanted to hear about it. But it is not difficult to draw important conclusions by analyzing the military situation. We do not need personal witness accounts to write that life for Tunisian Jews came to a halt. Everything they depended on collapsed within months; their French alliance was completely destroyed, relationships with their Islamist neighbors worsened beyond recognition and their sense of security was gone forever. Tunisian Muslims could not do much to help, as their enthusiasm towards the Axis Forces was unbearable. The same goes for the French. A large part of the Jewish population had adopted the French language and culture, only to confront, 75 years later, a strange colonial beast in the form of the anti-Jewish Vichy administration, which at times was worse than the Germans. The Spanish-Portuguese Jews of the Grana (Granada), who had been playing a role for centuries by enhancing trade and cultural relations with Italy and other European countries, found out how miserable their link was as well. It did not take them long to figure out that Italy had turned to fascism. From 1940 to the end of the occupation, they invested all their energies turning to the Italian fascists for salvation from the German final solution, a last attempt to avoid extermination. The Turkish Bey monarch ruling Tunisia at the time was helpless, considering the centuries of underdevelopment in the country. All told, the Jews of Tunisia were colonized by Islam, the French, the Turkish Sultan, German Nazis and Italian Fascists—all at the same time. They became completely alienated from the economic and cultural networks with the local population, built over many centuries. It is also important to remember that the majority of Tunisian Jews were heavily taxed and most were relatively poor to begin with, and were only beginning to enjoy a new level of prosperity. Still, the Germans managed to levy collective fines estimated at 100 million francs, not including the lootings in Djerba and elsewhere. They shipped to Germany anything of value, from furniture to books and jewelry, stripping the community of its wealth, and more importantly, its ancient past.

Freedman captures the essence of the war when he writes that recent evidence proved that the North African Campaign was not "a clean one" nor was it a "legend." He continues: "Rommel himself was no racial fanaticist, but he paved the way for the machinery of destruction with his victories," ignoring completely the consequences of his campaign.

There is one Tunisian Muslim mentioned in Yad Vashem (holocaust Memorial in Jerusalem) as helping some Jews escape from the Germans. This same person was also reported by members of his family to have hosted German soldiers who had run away from the battlefield at the end of the war. He had a large farm and was visited by a journalist who tried to get more information on the incident. The journalist was told by a member of the family not to mention the affair to farm workers, for fear of repercussions. There are other stories told by Tunisian Jews of Muslims helping Jews in Tunisia. But in general, Muslims followed their Islamic teachings, coated with anti-colonialist sentiment, against the French and the English. Tunisian nationalists never viewed its Jews as an indigenous part of the country's population, and thus Islamic anti-colonial nationalism in the 1940s had no place for anyone who was not Muslim. By the time the war ended, Tunisia was in ruins and its people devastated. The Arabs were never taken to task for implementing "Nuremberg-style" policies that resulted in the ethnic cleansing of its Jewish people because there was no government to take to task. Some have recently called for the declaration of the King of Morocco as a Righteous Gentile for his part in saving Jews. Apparently, he is said to have saved 200,000 Jews, most of whom were later made to leave for Israel and other countries. However, Yad Vashem does not list King Mohammed V in their database of the righteous among nations. In fact, no Muslim is listed anywhere in this database. There was also a German soldier who saved a few young Tunisian Jews by releasing them from prison. At the end of the war this soldier visited the family of one of the released prisoners asking for refuge trying to avoid becoming a prisoner of war. He was hidden by them and smuggled out of Tunisia a few years later. He said he was not a Nazi, and the Tunisian Jewish family was the only family he had throughout the rest of his life.

It is important to remember that the Nazis and Fascists in Tunisia were busy trying to win a war that from the outset they knew they were losing. This explains why the majority of Jews were spared. It is equally important to remember that Tunisia was not really under occupation. It was a theater of war, and the country as whole was swallowed by a vicious modern military operation unequalled in history. There was really no time for the Germans to concern themselves with the details of occupation, as was the case in some European countries. There was no meaningful internal opposition whatsoever to their presence in the country; the local population basically did not count in the grand German scheme of things. However, the local population in Tunisia did not embrace the Germans and the Italians. And, it is more accurate to say that no one really understood then (as now) the magnitude of the war around them. Most Tunisian Jews had no idea what the Western world was about to do on their lands and to their lives. They were witnessing the last breath of colonial Europe.

The Germans could not break the centuries-old bonds of the people in Tunisia, at least not in the first few years of the war. Tunisia had somehow withstood every invader throughout its history, and it managed to survive the Nazis. But after the war, internal Islamist nationalists were able to carry out what invaders were unable to execute throughout Tunisia's history: the elimination of all minorities, including its indigenous Jewish population. Islamist nationalists in Tunisia implemented the final solution, exiling its Jews from their lands with nearly 100 percent success.

Karin Albou has created an impossible scenario in a movie called Le chant des mariées, which deals with friendship between poor Muslim and Jewish girls during the German occupation of Tunis. Albou has done her research, and her film touches on many issues from a personal perspective; it is a beautiful and brilliant portrayal of the time that allows young Tunisian Jews and Muslims alike a taste of their shared history.

Towards the end of the Tunisian Campaign in May 1943, the Germans simply gave up and stopped following orders down the chain of command. They only had enough supplies and ammunition to continue fighting for a few more days. They could have stalled the enemy from their assault on Italy and Europe, but instead they just quit by the thousands. They were well trained, well fed professional soldiers, and they just "piled into motorcycles and trucks and drove to the nearest prison stockade."[47] The Allied Forces were glad, but also completely surprised at their behavior. The might of the German army collapsed so unexpectedly and so rapidly that the Allied command was worried that their forces would become over-confident in the fights ahead. Tunisia had worked its magic once again.

Years later, after being silent all this time, a few Tunisian Jews decided that their plight during the occupation was not properly recorded in Yad Vashem. Their modest grievances toward the Israeli State revolved around their suffering during WWII at the hands of the Germans and Italians, and their life under Allied bombardment. Once again, Tunisian Jews had been drawn into a false historical narrative, adapting a European perspective within the Zionist project in order to understand their current miserable situation. Yosi Reuven, a 74-year-old from Be'er Sheva working alone in his small room, was driven by the quest to shed a bit of light and do some justice to those who were killed during this period. He was able to put together a list of 600 names of Tunisian Jews who perished during that period. The silence here screams louder, not just because history was ignored by everyone in Israel and Tunisia, but also because of the absence of numbers and statistics about how many died at the time and what their suffering meant during and after this period. The Holocaust, after all, was not just a European event.

Interestingly, Hirschberg and his co-authors, in writing their famous historical account of Tunisia, brought the son of Rabbi Kahlfon in Djerba as a witness to what happened to the Tunisian community during the German occupation. According to him, he heard nothing and saw nothing (not unusual for a Rabbi or son of a Rabbi, even in Israel) for seven months. These Israeli historians spent two pages telling his non-story, yet they brushed aside the US Council General's account of Tunisia in the previous century as irrelevant. A detailed and honest account of Tunisia and its Jewish population during the Second World War has yet to be written... It has not been told.

Every year survivors of the Tunisian Holocaust meet as part of the History Society of Tunisian Jews (Société d'Histoire des Juifs de Tunisie) at the Shoa Memorial in Paris. Very few are still alive, but their story was recounted year after year. Their story is of the persecution of Jews under Walther Rauff from November 1942 to May 1943. Very little is said about the previous two years under Vichy, a period which was no less destructive. Meetings like this were held in living rooms around the world wherever Tunisians were living. I have been present at a few of these gathering, and not once did anyone mention the gold that everyone seems to be looking for in Corsican beaches. Attending the 70th meeting in Paris in 2013 were Ms. Bertinotti, Minister of Social Affairs, the Mayor of Paris Bertrand

Delanoë, diplomatic representatives of Tunisia and Israel in France, Joel Mergui and Richard Prasquier, President of the CRIF, and various civil and religious leaders. They were commemorating the roundup of Jews in Tunis by the SS (on December 9, 1942) and the establishment of labor camps on Tunisian territory.

The chairman of this year's meeting was the Chief Rabbi of France, Gilles Bernheim. They read the known names of Tunisian Jews who died in the Field of Honor, Jews deported, Jews in European camps, and those murdered in labor camps established by the Nazis in Tunisia. According to Claude Nataf, President of the SHJT: "Il y raflait les Juifs avant de les envoyer dans des camps de travail, prélude à une élimination physique programmée." [The Jews were rounded up and send to work camps, a prelude to their planned physical elimination."] Nataf and other speakers kept stating that they did not understand what had happened but that they must at least remember. This period has been ignored and misunderstood for many years. Historians in Israel and France have been baffled by the ignorance and the inability to interpret the events that took place in Tunisia – not just the Nazi occupation but also the effect this all has had on the fabric of North African society as a whole, effects that we are still witnessing today across the Arab world. This part of the story is explained in a separate book I wrote called Silencing the Past: The Arab Spring, Israel and the Jews of Tunisia.

The present follow-up book attempts to further put the puzzle together, by focusing on understanding what is behind the stories of gold treasure.

By the end of the war the Jews of Tunisia were left with no gold, no personal wealth and no property, as their businesses were also confiscated, beginning in 1940 – and thus no memory remains of their history and participation in the development of North African society. A whole community started from scratch elsewhere, learning to adapt to new situations and new environments without understanding their past. No one counted them, and they did not count – neither in Israel nor in France.

Indeed, their ordeal had started two years earlier. The first Bey's decree of anti-Jewish laws in Tunisia was signed on November 30, 1940; it imposes numerous restrictions on the public service and the professions, with provisional administrators controlling Jewish businesses, a ban on doctors from practicing with non-Jews, and the dissolution of Jewish organizations. This decree was applied to "all Tunisian Jews whose three grandparents were of the Jewish race or two grandparents of the same race if the spouse is himself Jewish." However, the most anti-sematic laws came not from the Germans, but the French who controlled Tunisia, and the Bey who in turn worked for them. The Jewish population of Tunisia (and Libya) was in a panic mode for almost three years.

They had no idea what was in store for them from the colonial world. The situation they found themselves in was extremely confusing. Two colonial powers were struggling for control of Tunisia, the French and the Italians, and later the English, the Germans and the Americans.

We should recall that at the outset of WWII there were over 120,000 Italians living in Tunisia. The city of 'la Goulet' was built by Sicilian and Corsican Tunisians. A Tunisian Jew in all of this had to speak Italian, French, Arabic, Berber and Hebrew in order to just get by. The flow of the Jewish population from Tunisia to all quarters of the world coincided with the disappearance of the Italians living in Tunisia as well. Jews, Italians, Maltese and others disappeared from Tunisia, which is today completely Muslim and mostly Arab. Christians were made to leave Tunisia, too. For years the Italians viewed Tunisia as an "Italian territory governed by the French." The French, on the other hand, held on to their Protectorate/Colony imposing the French language everywhere. Still, the Italians had their own newspapers, and some were waiting for a power shift, especially for Libya to be overtaken by Italy. In any event, the Italian presence was also what prevented the extermination of the Jewish population in Tunisia by the Germans. Corsica, Sardinia and especially Sicily viewed Tunisia as an alternative home when things went wrong in Italy. Often for trading and other reasons, families settled in Tunisia in order to expand connections, trade and territorial control. One of the leading mafia heads in the US, Carlos Marcello, was a Tunisian born of Sicilian origin. Many of the Italians in Tunisia could trace their family origin to the Middle Ages and even before. In fact, in 1640 a Corsican-born Tunisian tax collector and his decedents ruled Tunisia for almost one hundred years. The Italian Tunisians, Corsicans and Sicilians had something in common, which helped save lives in the Jewish community, the Omertà. This code of silence was a guiding behavioral policy that prevented the various powers from interfering too much with the affairs of the community. It was not just a term used by the mafia. It simply meant that information about individuals and communities should not be transferred to any government –especially not to any occupying government. This tactic was widely used during the Nazi occupation of Tunisia, and the Germans were helpless in combating it; they did not know it existed. Thousands of Tunisian Jews were saved through the use of this code. In Corsica, thousands of Jews were hidden by villagers, and almost none were passed to Nazi hands. The official stand was that there were no Jews on the island.[48] They furnished these Jewish refugees with false papers and the code of silence worked its magic – thousands were saved this way. Employees of the Corsican authority were also sworn to this code and would not disclose the presence of Jews on the island. Michael Cosgrove calls the whole story the "irony of Omertà." Also, the Corsicans kept quiet when it came to finding information on Rommel's treasure, if it existed. They were not going to provide French or Italian authorities information concerning the whereabouts of the treasure.

At the beginning of WWII, the Germans entered France, and Vichy military government control was instituted in Tunisia and with it a series of anti-Jewish decrees designed to curtail Jewish hold on the Tunisian economy. The decrees were also designed to restrict the Italian population of Tunisia. The decree to adopt French everywhere as the official state language was accepted without much resistance. But anti-business laws towards the Jewish population affected the whole community. By 1940 the city of Tunis was a European city for all intents and purposes. It was populated by 75,000 French, 120,000 Italians and over 70,000 Jews. The latter was composed of one third Italian, some Jews of Spanish and Portuguese decent; the rest were Berber, the original inhabitants of the country.

These divisions within the Tunisian Jewish community were fully manifest in full force during the Nazi occupation. The Nazis assigned community leaders with providing lists of thousands of people to work in various work camps. They drew the lists without hesitation, but "forgetting" to enlist their family and friends, and thus effectively becoming an identical version of the Judenrat in the ghettos of Europe. The lists thus excluded the upper echelons of the community, their relatives and intellectuals in society. Albert Memi has written a whole book about his experience in one of those camps, including the above-mentioned fissures within the community. Memi was a philosopher and not an historian, but his account is fully relevant to our story in this context. He apparently joined the list of his own free will, in solidarity with the regular folks who were plunged into an unknown situation.

THE ISRAELI CONNECTION?

It seemed that every government around the world was interested in ex-Nazis and what they had to offer. Governments in Latin America opened their arms and provided conditions for them to prosper and become model citizens. Governments in the Arab world were also more than eager to hire consultants and engineers who were publically known as Nazis, and some were even high on the list of Nazis hunters. The CIA and the FBI have their own story of employing these individuals in the US. Many of these former Nazis were "aggressively recruited" at the height of the Cold War, as many of the recruits were considered "anti-Soviet assets." "They believed the ex-Nazis' intelligence value against the Russians outweighed what one official called 'moral lapses' in their service to the Third Reich. The agency hired one former SS officer as a spy in the 1950s, for instance, even after concluding he was probably guilty of 'minor war crimes.'"[49]

However, many of these individuals were not just guilty of minor crimes but of atrocities over long periods, and not just against Jews. Eric Lichtblau, of The New York Times, claimed that the CIA concealed information about these activities and continues to do so even today.

The question of Argentina's gold reserves being linked to the Third Reich is also interesting, as it was among only a very few number of nations which saw their gold reserves climb during the war before falling, or in some instances remaining high, like Switzerland. Bolivia was another country that fell under scrutiny and asset freezing action by the US during World War II.[50]

Argentina's Gold Reserves (BIS Annual Accounts) 1935 – 1949) US$m

Year	US$m
1935	444
1936	501
1937	469
1938	431
1939	466
1940	353
1941	--
1942	--
1943	939
1944	1,111
1945	1,351
1946	1,185
1947	319

However, the Israeli connection in this affair, which directly relates to our subject, is scandalous and stands out more than any of the Latin American connections. A few Israeli historians claimed that Walther Rauff, the man responsible for the total destruction of the Tunisian Jewish community, was apparently working for the Israelis, as a spy in Syria. Rauff was only man who knew where Rommel's treasure was hidden but he was never interrogated on this question by anyone. The journalists bring up a CIA Memorandum from March 24, 1950 that revealed this atrocious relationship. When the Nazi-hunter Beate Klarsfeld heard of this she was indeed shocked and became speechless. The same man who was responsible for the death of hundreds of thousands of people was said to be on a Jewish payroll in the years following Israel's independence, a "Nazi in the service of the Jewish State?| According to these reports he apparently was not the only one. Klarsfeld spent years tracking Rauff in Chile. She demonstrated and even got arrested for it by the Chilean police, and was now learning about the harsh world of Middle East politics.

During Passover in 1993, Israeli journalist Shlomo Nakdimon published an interview with Shalhevet Freier in Yedioth Ahronoth (an Israeli daily newspaper). In late 1940s Mr. Freier was a branch director at the Foreign Ministry's Political Department, and in the 1970s he chaired the Israel Atomic Energy Commission. He died in 1995. In this interview he related how he had recruited Walther Rauff in Italy, after friends in the Italian Foreign Ministry tipped him off about the new arrival of a former SS soldier. (Rauff was using an alias at the time.) According to Freier, it was the Political Department that employed Rauff.[51] Also in 1993, Haaretz published an article titled "Our Man in Damascus," by Shraga Elam and Dennis Whitehead. Apparently, Rauff was not an exception, as the employment of former Nazis in the service of Israel's intelligence service was designed to extract information in Arab neighboring countries. Rauff was intended to be sent to Egypt, but when that did not materialize he was sent to Syria. It should be noted that both Syria and Egypt employed many ex-Nazis.

Israelis, it seems, were keen on German Nazis operating as spies. In Egypt, Wolfgang Lotz is probably one of the country's most famous spies. Lotz was not a Nazi but an Israeli of German descent who pretended to be a Nazi. In 1959, he was sent by the Israeli intelligence to Germany to build a cover story for himself as a German businessman with a shady Nazi past, including being an officer of the Wehrmacht who participated in the North African war with the Axis Forces. Lotz would later travel to Egypt to build an equestrian school. In 1960, he began establishing connections with high-ranking political and military officials. In 1965, he was arrested for espionage and released with the help of West Germany's intelligence agency. He admitted working for the Israelis on Egyptian public television but continued to keep his fake identity story until his release. His son Oded Gur Arie wrote a book called The Champaign Spy, which was later turned into a documentary. Interestingly, Arie became a target in the 1973 Yom Kippur War. The Egyptians apparently knew he was on the border, and the Israelis feared an Egyptian commando raid to kidnap him. Soldiers in his unit were warned not to talk about Lotz or his son on their radios. What Israelis did not know was that Egyptians and the Syrian intelligence services were in close cooperation for a number of years.

The same year another Israeli spy, Eli Cohen, was captured in Syria. Lotz and Eli Cohen were using similar spy transmission equipment. However, Eli Cohen, who managed to become the Chief Adviser to the Minister of Defense in Syria, was convicted as an Israeli spy and was hanged by the Syrians. His cover story while in Syria was that he was a Syrian businessman who lived in Argentina and was returning home. The only problem was that hardly any Syrians returned home from Argentina. For Christian and Muslim Arabs, Argentina was a one-way ticket destination, as well as for former Nazis. Israeli intelligence reported that valuable information was transmitted from Egypt and Syria, which helped Israel win the 1967 war. All this is doubtful considering that Israel's intelligence did not know about Egyptian and Syrian plans of a synchronized attack in 1973, the only real war in Israel's history. The war was a tragic surprise for everyone in Israel. Two large armies prepared for war, for years, mobilizing their full resources, and no one in Israel knew. Such reliance on spies to deliver such obvious war activities within both Egypt and Syria proved to be useless. All they had to do was embark on a political analysis and interview regular soldiers at the Bar Lev Line to find out that Egypt was planning an attack. The price of misunderstanding the region was high in the 1950s, as the entire indigenous Jewish population was ordered out of Egypt. On Nasser's orders, more than 100,000 Egyptian Jews were pushed out, never to come to back, penniless and heartbroken.

But back to Walther Rauff... Elam and Whitehead claim that in 1950 Rauff was in Syria, working as an advisor to President Hosni Zaim. When Zaim was deposed in a military coup, Rauff was rushed out of Syria and was helped by the Israelis to resettle in Ecuador, and later in Chile. Why? This turn of events makes very little sense. Why would the Israelis enlist him, and why would they help him escape to South America? There are no easy answers to this, and so many questions. Did he deliver Tunisian and other gold to the Israelis in exchange for his life? For years Rauff was a wanted man after the war. His name came up 31 times during the Nuremberg Trials, and he was considered as the man responsible for the mobile gas chambers and the deaths of at least 100,000 people, possibly even 200,000. He was directly responsible for thousands of deaths and other atrocities in Tunisia. He was high up on Nazi-hunters' lists. In fact, he was considered one of the top three most-wanted Nazi criminals. The German Ingelligence had a 900 pages file on Rauff war time activities. What was the intelligence service in Israel thinking? Curiously, what information could Rauff deliver that was of such paramount importance? Was his life valued in tons of gold? Was Israel involved in finding Rommel's gold?

His activities in destroying the Tunisian Jewish community were not mentioned in any of the published reports, and it is also probable that no one at the time knew (or cared to know) about his activities there. He was heading the Einsatzkommando in Tunisia. In July 1943 he was stationed in Corsica, and in September of that same year in Milan, where he continued to hold the reputation of a ruthless Gestapo officer. At the end of the war he barely escaped being lynched by the locals in Milan. He was arrested in 1945, and escaped from prison in 1947.[52] He was only person who would know where the stolen gold was hidden. He was the person who organized the looting of Tunisian wealth, leaving a long trail of destruction. He was the only one who could confirm the number of shipments made with looted gold from Tunisia to Germany. Rauff was the man who could confirm Rommel's participation in the actual lootings. But no one seemed interested in asking him these questions. The subject of looted gold and his cruelty in Tunisia was not mentioned in any of the leaked CIA or Israeli intelligence reports. Fleig, the young soldier, heard stories about the treasure while in prison, but it was Rauff who implemented the melting of gold into bullion while still in Tunisia. He was the key person to know whether or not the treasure lie at the bottom of the ocean off the coast of Corsica. It seemed that the Israelis did not care to find out more about this part of the story, or for that matter any story about Jews of North Africa. Nazi-hunters concentrated their efforts into trying to extradite Rauff from Chile to Germany, pointing to his part in the extermination of tens of thousands of Jews in Europe. The different governments in Chile did not cooperate and refused to arrest him, stating that he was a model citizen in the country for many years and had not committed any crime while living there. After all, governments in Latin America did not invite German Nazis because of their blue eyes, disciplined behavior or technological knowhow. There was money involved – gold, and lots of it. What other motivation could they have had to refuse extraditing Rauff? Laws in Chile did not prevent such an arrest which was based on past atrocities. How much gold was involved that prevented his extradition? How much gold did it take for him to become a law-abiding citizen?

Elam and Whitehead claimed that the Israeli agent Edmond (Ted) Cross wanted Rauff in Egypt. The same source outlined in a report that Rauff did not reach Egypt, but the American Ambassador to Egypt at the time reported in 1953 of a Nazi named Rauff in Cairo. Cross was recruited by Asher Ben-Natan in 1948, who was then Director of Operations of the Foreign Ministry's political department (before the establishment of the "Mossad"). Cross was fluent in several languages and worked for the British intelligence during the Second World War. According to an article by Gil Meltzer in Yedioth Ahronoth, "Cross was part of the Gross family, a wealthy Jewish family in Budapest." According to Meltzer, he financed his extravagant lifestyle through drug trafficking and offered his services to the Egyptians, who paid him 20,000 dollars, which was then an enormous sum. When the Israelis found this out he was arrested, convicted and sent to serve a long sentence. After his release he went into the restaurant business and among other things founded the "Wimpy" burger chain in Israel.

In later life, interviewed by a German reporter in Chile, Walther Rauff went on record: "Did I think twice about employing the gas vans? I couldn't say. At the time the most important consideration for me was the psychological stress felt by the men involved in the shootings. This problem was overcome by the use of gas vans."[53] In the same interview he stated that he tried to present an extermination plan of the Jews of North Africa to Rommel while he was in Libya. Rommel apparently rejected the idea.

Ruth Kimche, a former Mossad employee, wrote that the original plan was to send Cross to Egypt in order to assassinate some key government figures. The plan was not executed, but while he was in Egypt Cross fell in love with an Egyptian Princess, Amina Nur a-Din. On his return to Israel he decided that Rauff would be sent instead. According to Elam and Whitehead in the Haaretz article; "From Damascus Rauff went to Beirut, and from there to Italy. With the assistance of Israeli, and apparently also British intelligence, he sailed for South America in December 1949."

This story only recently became explosive on Internet forums, raising eyebrows and many questions. Here is a sample reaction from one of them: "Mossad made use of Rauff in Syria and then helped him to escape, that even though he murdered hundreds of thousands of Jews? And you dismiss this as normal procedure? May heaven help you. After the Syrian thing Rauff was of no further use to Mossad and surely they would have killed him, or made a spectacle of him by dragging him to court." The story is indeed incomprehensible, leading to serious allegations and to obvious conspiracy theories of all kinds.

We may never know the real story of Rauff and the Israeli connection. We can only speculate that the gold connection in this story may be logical and probably the only explanation available. Only gold and greed could have made Rauff a free man.

The Nazi hunter Beate Klarsfeld had a hard time believing that Israel had something to do with the situation that allowed Rauff to avoid trial or extradition to West Germany. Klarsfeld kept up the pressure for years in the United States, trying to influence American public opinion to help convince the governments of Chile and Paraguay to extradite the wanted war criminals living there. Walther Rauff resided in Chile, and Joseph Mengele in Paraguay; both were responsible for murder and atrocities committed to Jews and non-Jews during World War II. (Mengele was the doctor who carried out inhumane experiments on prisoners at the Auschwitz death camp.) "What we can do in the case of Rauff is to mobilize public opinion," Klarsfeld told a news conference at the headquarters of the American Jewish Committee. In suggesting that the U.S. apply pressure on the government of President Augusto Pinochet, Klarsfeld said "dictatorships are always sensitive to pressure coming from abroad." (Jewish Telegraphic Agency 1984) It did not work, despite the pressure, and Rauff remained a "model citizen" in Chile.

There are also reports that in 1958 Rauff worked for the BND (West Germany's International Intelligence Service), and there are even indications that the British Intelligence was also involved. Others claimed that he was later on the payroll of the Intelligence Agency in Chile. Rauff, it seems, was in high demand, and he probably was serving more than one master. According to Geraldine Schwarz, in a recent French documentary "Rome devient une plateforme pour l'exfiltration des nazis en fuite" [Rome had become a platform for the ex-filtration of Nazi fugitives], indicating that Rauff was also connected with the Vatican. The Vatican in this report became a center for Nazi fugitives who needed to integrate into society in whatever capacity. Quite a few ex-Nazis opened offices in this City State, providing their services to the highest bidder. Schwarz, however, does not mention the Israeli connection. Instead, she indicates without reservation that Rauff was recruited by the Syrians in order to institute a Gestapo-type organization with respect to treatment of Jews in Syria and other opposition groups.

There is no logic at all to reports that Rauff was working for the Germans, Israelis, Egyptians, British and Syrians and even the Americans all at the same time. In a Chilean television interview, Rauff, while waiting for a decision on his extradition, seemed assured he would be set free. Speaking in English, Rauff did not claim his innocence, though he was certain that the Pinochet government would treat him like every other respectable citizen. For some reason, every interview, article or documentary on Rauff – in English, Spanish or German – lacked the historical rigor to confront him with serious questions. Hundreds of ex-Nazis attended his funeral in 1984, and many gave the traditional Nazi salute to their comrade, all in front of Chilean public media. Jerry Meldon from Tufts University explained in part that the calm façade Rauff was projecting was due to "Operation Sunrise," which permitted scores of Nazi criminals to escape the courts. Recently, archived materials suggest collaborations between Allied intelligence services and former Nazis who stepped forward. "Ex-Nazis were everywhere" Der Spiegel's staff wrote: "Not just politicians and public servants, at least not in the early years of the Republic. Senior members of the media, including at Spiegel, proved to be unwilling or incapable of sounding the alarm. This isn't surprising, given the number of ex-Nazis who had forced their way into editorial offices."[54] The Bild tabloid newspaper published an article in 2011 exposing that Rauff was employed by the German Intelligence Agency and was paid 70,000 Marks for his services. Historian Martin Cueppers of the University of Stuttgart told Bild: "Documents show that a complete club of Nazi insiders formed itself here in the BND. All this was happening while the Federal Republic of Germany was increasing its hunt for Nazi war criminals."[55]

Back in Tunisia, Ben Ali, the ousted President was said to flee the country with his wife and with over one and half tons of gold bullion to the safe haven of the Arab Emirates. Tunisian authorities were asking for extradition and were unsuccessful. The Ben Ali family continues to live in that country. Gold, especially when in quantity, appears to have its own persuasive language and magic that governments everywhere understand. The couple was said to have approached the Tunisian central bank, requesting that the gold be loaded onto a plane. The personnel in the bank refused at first but very quickly followed instructions. Once the gold was loaded the couple took off to their new safe haven. The new government in power searched their various houses for treasures only to find valuable archeological artifacts everywhere they looked. The chief archeologist was said to have cried on seeing this level of archeological looting by the country's political leaders. The Tunisian past was stolen over and over again; from the Arab invasion to Turkish colonialism, French colonialism, German and Italian occupations, and most recently the new Beys (Turkish Sultans) and radical Islamists of all kinds who saw everything in Tunisia as their own personal property. The story is similar in Libya and other countries of North Africa and the Middle East.

The real story in North Africa was not just how the Allied Forces won the war there but how the whole of North Africa became Arab in character, cleansed of its indigenous Jewish inhabitants. Nazi objectives in North Africa were the same as those in Europe. Once planted, the seeds of destruction could not be stopped, and the targeted people once again were the Jews of the region, who disappeared forever. I'm probably the only person arguing that the ongoing turmoil in North Africa and the Middle East is precisely because the Arabs did away with their Jewish indiginous population.

Latin American countries became preferred host countries for Nazis. Rauff first landed in Ecuador and later settled in Chile. According to secret CIA documents, he was helped by Israeli secret agents, even after his mission in Syria. How he was recruited as an Israeli agent is beyond the scope of this book. A detailed account of the fiasco surrounding his engagement will not be discussed because it does not matter. The Israelis are well known for misunderstanding political realities. For years, Israeli political leaders appeared to have a major disability when it came to understanding Jews from Arab-conquered lands of North Africa and the Middle East. Hence, they had a problem understanding the countries of the Arab world. Everyone in the region who spoke Arabic was for them an Arab and was therefore either an enemy or part of a "lower Jewish class." This major disability was also what led Israel to be unprepared for the Yom Kippur War. We will probably never know the full truth about those involved in the Rauff fiasco. What is certain is that no one will be held accountable for it. In fact, the person who is said to be responsible for hiring Walther Rauff was promoted and became a leading scientist and the chief of the Atomic Research Agency in Israel.

Three successive Chilean governments, under

Frei, Allende and Pinochet, declined to extradite Rauff. The German ambassador confirmed on March 5, 1984 that a formal request for extradition was made to the government of Chile. He was told by the foreign ministry that President Pinochet would not deport Rauff since he "had committed no crimes in Chile and that the statute of limitations had run out on the crime of murder for which has been accused in West Germany." There are other reports that between 1958 and 1962 Rauff worked for the Bundesnachrichtendienst, West Germany's intelligence service. In the late 1970s and 1980s, he was probably the most wanted Nazi fugitive still alive.

In their investigation, Elam and Whitehead report that the initial contact with Rauff was made by Shalheveth Freier, an Israeli scientist of German decent, born in 1920. Freier fled Germany in 1940 and interestingly and questionably, he also participated in the North African wars with the British. In 1970, he was appointed as the Director General of the Israel Atomic Energy Commission. In the 1973 October War (Yom Kippur) he was invited to a meeting with Golda Meir and Moshe Dayan to discuss the possible use of a nuclear display of force as a last resort. Freier claimed that he did not know of Rauff's past. When he asked Rauff about his activities during the war Rauff mentioned only that while in the Gestapo he was responsible for the production of counterfeit Pounds Sterling, in order to damage the British economy. Elam and Whitehead claimed that it is hard to believe that Shalheveth Freier did not know the full story of Rauff's past. Shalheveth, it was believed, was also responsible for recruiting another Jewish fellow named Jaac van Harten, who was apparently involved in counterfeiting money and collaborating with the Nazis. His family claimed he was a hero who helped many in Hungary. Ironically, Shalhevet is also the name of a Jewish youth science competition, "The Shalheveth Freier Physics Tournament". The theme of the 2013 competition was a "Safecracking Contest." Shalhevet is also the name of a non-profit organization for the physically disabled, named after the scientist who recruited the man who initially built gas vans for the disabled in Germany. The head of the foundation, Miriam Freier received the Israeli Humanitarian award in 2013. Freier was interviewed in 1966 by Nana Nosinov about Van Harten. Freier explained at length what he knew about the affair and how he assisted Van Harten throughout the post-war period. At the end of the interview he added that he approached Van Harten at his jewelry store in Tel Aviv for money for an electronic music lab he was running. Freier asked for a loan of 2,000 Lira ($550) and was turned down by Van Harten[56] (take 903).[57] Freire who was Israel's science attaché in Paris until 1960 became a few short years later the head of the Atomic Energy Commission in Israel. Freier was interviewed before his death about Israel's nuclear energy. According to him, England and France approached Israel in 1954 for help with designs and technological knowhow in building nuclear reactors. This kind of arrogance and outright deception about Israel's might at this point of history was indeed too much to swallow...

It is obvious that it is impossible to come up with the real story, considering not only the time that has passed since the last world war but also because of the complexity of the issues and the twisted relationships of many greedy individuals and governments involved. A Jewish Tunisian would tremble at the thought of Rauff working as a spy for Israel, for whatever purpose and for whatever information. It is also obvious that during the 1950s, Israel's leadership had little understanding of the Arab world and even less understanding of the Jews who came from the countries of North Africa and the Middle East. Still, the Rauff story, if true, is more than just a fiasco or error in judgment. No historian in Israel was or is ready to touch the story and the article published in Hebrew by a mainstream Israeli newspaper made little headlines. This is not surprising considering that we are still living in an era when North African Jews are not considered as having suffered from Nazi persecution.[58] The Holocaust Learning organization published a time-line of Jews persecuted by the Nazi; Tunisia is not mentioned in this list. The Wiesenthal Center for Holocaust Studies agrees that North African Jews were persecuted, but Tunisia is not mentioned among those countries whose Jews died in work camps: "The Jewish communities in North Africa were persecuted, but the

Jews in these countries were neither deported to the death camps, nor were they systematically murdered."[59] Obviously, none of this is true. The Jews of Tunisia were deported to work camps by the thousands, and many died either in these camps, from random shootings, deportation and rape, or casualties of Allied bombings. They were the only group singled out in Tunisia, forced to appoint a Judenrat, stripped of their wealth through taxes, fines, looting and rape – yet for years not one word has been mentioned in Holocaust history books. The history books used in Israeli schools has but one page on the history of Jews from North Africa and the Middle East. My argument here and elsewhere is that it is impossible to understand WWII without understanding what happened in Tunisia. It is impossible to understand the Holocaust without understanding what happened to the Jews of Tunisia. Is it therefore any wonder that no one is able to find "Rommel's treasure"?

Latin American escape routes for fugitive Nazis were called "ratlines." Immediately after the war thousands of Nazis used these routes to avoid trials for war crimes. The first route was from Germany to Spain and from there to South America. The other favorite route was to Italy and from there to either the Middle East or South America. Many also opted for the safe haven of North America and Canada. Companies, religious Institutions and governments of all sorts helped them escape. There was simply no way to halt this migration. The most that

Jews could do was to track prominent Nazis and uncover their crimes – and if lucky, bring them to justice. In the aftermath of the war, the relocation of Nazis became a business in itself. They were providing their expertise in various fields of military science and were thus in high demand during the Cold-War era. Others simply used bribes and business connections in return for a new safe home. In Chile the community was comfortable enough to continue their allegiance to Hitler and to Nazism.

A Nazi corporal by the name of Paul Schaefer even founded a sect in southern Chile, creating there a well-fortified state within a state. Child abuse, brainwashing, drugs and other horrific activities took place there. The place was called the Colonia Dignidad, surrounded by electrified fences and armed guards everywhere, and it was operated as a cult based on Nazi ideology. The site later became a perfect place for the interrogation and torture of those opposed to Pinochet. It was left to operate under the full knowledge of the regime, including the Chief of Intelligence, General Manuel Contreras, who was often seen visiting. Most Nazis, however, integrated quite well into the society in each country that hosted them.

The big question remains: how many Nazis and much gold were imported to Latin America and elsewhere? There are no easy answers. In 1997 a five-person presidential commission was set up in Brazil to try and answer these questions, as well as figure out what happened to the funds Nazis brought with them. It took the commission 18 months to conclude the investigation. One of those investigated was Albert Blume, a German-born member of the Nazi Party in Brazil. After his death in 1983, his Brazilian bank deposit box revealed a small treasure worth millions, containing watches, rings, gold bars and gold teeth. Nevertheless, the task of finding billions of dollars in looted gold smuggled out of Germany's vaults has proven to be a difficult task that continues to intrigue many researchers. It largely remains an open question...

CONCLUSION

"But perhaps we are looking at this story from the wrong angle?" This question triggered the writing of this book, which has attempted to explore the various arguments as to why we cannot find Rommel's treasure. Elsewhere, a similar statement was published by a frustrated treasure hunter: "Interesting stories! I fear we might be waiting a while longer since that last story was from 2007 and no word yet." The most common versions of the story share inaccurate and partial information of what the treasure is and where it is buried. The direction I have taken is different, and hopefully I have contributed even a little to the ongoing discussion and quest for the missing treasure. I'm convinced that the gold looted in Tunisia became Nazi gold, and its storage and usage was no different than other looted gold that ended in vaults and banks everywhere. The bulk of Nazi looting in Tunisia occurred in early 1943. Any other individual looting was simply an extension of the real treasure looted over a period of seven months in Tunisia, and much longer in Libya. The six chests supposedly containing the treasure would thus represent only a very small part of what was looted in Tunisia. The big treasure has spread around the world, and with it thousands of years of history. This period led to the elimination of a civilization that ceased to exist as a result of looting and other incomprehensible and horrible events. The main treasure was collected by Walther Rauff on the orders of Rommel and the Third Reich. The plot thus thickens, and with it conspiracy theories of all kinds involving international espionage, the Cold War, Middle Eastern politics – and at the heart of it all, gold.

Notes

1. Nicholas Köhler, "The Bank of Canada's Move, and What It Means for a Fabled Underground Vault," Mclean's, June 11, 2013.

2. Adam Lebor, "How Six Months before WWII Britain Gave Hitler $9-million in Gold (that Belonged to Another Country)," The Telegraph, August 1, 2013.

3. Forbes, 2014

4. Jan Bart Gewald, "Gold The True Motor Of West African History: An Overview Of The Importance Of Gold In West Africa And Its Relations With The Wider World," The Rosenberg Quarterly Magazine, 2010.

5. Alex Newman, "Gadhafi's Gold-money Plan Would Have Devastated Dollar," The New American, November 11, 2011.

6. Leen Bultinck, "Belgian Gold in Foreign Hands," National Bank of Belgium Museum, www.nbbmuseum.be/2010/03/belgische-goud.htm.

7. Mr. Mervyn Jones Mr. Philippe Malo Ms. Anne De Derse, 57. Final Report, Tripartite Commission for the Restitution of Monetary Gold, Brussels. September 13, 1998.

8. Jewish Restitution Successor Organization, Wikipedia, en.wikipedia.org/wiki/Jewish_Restitution_Successor_Organization.

9. Weekly Coompilation of Presidential Documents, vol. 34 (1998): Feb. 13, www.gpo.gov/fdsys/pkg/WCPD-1998-03-30/content-detail.html

10. Greg Bradsher, "Nazi Gold: The Merkers Mine Treasure," Prologue Magazine, vol. 31, no. 1 (Spring 1999).

11 Claude Nataf, "Allocution du Président de la SHJT," Harissa Magazine, March 2011.

12 "Messerschmitt Me 323," Wikipedia, en.wikipedia.org/wiki/Messerschmitt_Me_323.

13 Chris Parsons, "Nazi Leviathan Unearthed after 70 Years: Divers Discover Wreckage of 'Giant' German Luftwaffe Transport Plane Shot Down by British Fighter while Flying from Base in Sardinia," Daily Mail, October 3, 2012.

14 New York Times, 1958.

15 Tyler Durden, "Tunisia Central Bank Admits It Is Missing 1.5 Tons Of Gold," Zerohedge, January 2011.

16 Ruth Bond, Evening Standard, Trove, Digital Library of Australia, August 21, 1952.

17 Chicago Tribune, August 17, 1952.

18 Henry Samuel, "Rommel's Sunken Gold 'Found' by British Expert," Telegraph July 18, 2007.

19 "Nazi Gold," Wikipedia, en.wikipedia.org/wiki/Nazi_gold.

20 Kwame Opoku, "Memorandum on the Loot from Maqdala," An Ethiopian Journal, September 2008, tseday.wordpress.com/tag/british-empire/

21 "AFROMET," Wikipedia, en.wikipedia.org/wiki/AFROMET.

22 Richard Pankhurst, "The Story of Ethiopian Looted Crowns," Link Ethiopia.

23 Peter Allen, "Could a Wartime Photo Help Locate Looted Nazi Gold Worth £20m?" Daily Mail, July 21, 2007.

24 Dagblad van het Noorden.

25 Christian Spook, "Vatican Crimes in Croatia: Genocide, Bombings, Money Laundering, Forgery Exposed," christianspooksite.

wordpress.com/2014/01/05/vatican-crimes-in-croatia-genocide-bombings-money-laundering-forgery-exposed-2.

26 Max Gross, "Egyptian Scholar Planning Lawsuit Over Exodus Gold," The Jewish Daily Forward, August 29, 2003.

27 Samuel Kurinsky, "Gold and Silver Smithing: A Judaic Tradition Part I - The Near-East and the Mediterranean," The Hebrew History Federation, www.hebrewhistory.info/ factpapers/fp017-1_gold.htm.

28 Eizenstat Special Briefing on Nazi Gold. Stuart Eizenstat, US State Department, 2 June 1998. From "Nazi gold," Wikipedia.

29 Steve Weizman, "Tunisian Jews Win Holocaust claim," USA Today. February 11, 2008.

30 The Comet, December 5, 1926.

31 "Tunisian Campaign," National Museum of the US Airforce, October 2009, www.nationalmuseum.af.mil/ factsheets/factsheet_print.asp?fsID=1735&page=1.

32 Frederick Cooper, Colonialism in Question (Berkeley: University of California Press, 2005).

33 Haim Zeev Hirschberg, Eliezer Bashan and Robert Attal, A History of the Jews in North Africa, Vol. 2: From the Ottoman Conquests to the Present Time (Brill, 1997).

34 www.jstor.org.ezproxy.bibl.ulaval.ca/stable/pdfplus/3777449.pdf.

35 Donald J. Roberts II, "Raid on Rommel's Railroad in Tunisia During World War II," World War II Magazine, November 2000.

36 Kefteji, "Memorial Day in Tunisia: Bittersweet patriotism," May 2012, kefteji.wordpress.com/2012/05/28/memorial-day-in-tunisia-bittersweet-patriotism/.

37 Montreal Gazette, May 1943.

38 Montreal Gazette, May 1943.

39 Gary Aminoff, "Islamic Fascism: The Nazi Connection," American Thinker, December 11, 2012, www.american thinker.com/articles/2012/12/islamic_fascism_the_nazi_connection.html.

40 Jeffrey Herf. Nazi Propaganda for the Arab World (New Haven: Yale University Press, 2009).

41 Ashraf Amin, 339.

42 Carl Brown, "'Mon Ami' Hooker Doolittle: Early American Contacts with Habib Bourguiba" (Middle East Institute, 2004).

43 Jeffery Brainard, "Patton Tank Marks Suggest a Long Recovery," Science News, vol. 154, no. 6 (1998).

44 www.archives.gov/publications/prologue/1999/spring/nazi-gold-merkers-mine-treasure.html.

45 "Erwin Rommel Documentary," YouTube, November 12, 2013, www.youtube.com/watch?v=63uVhYrKOSU.

46 "German Prisoners of War in the United States," Wikipedia, en.wikipedia.org/wiki/German_prisoners_of_war_in_the_United_States.

47 Excerpts from "The German Soldier," Infantry Journal, Lone Sentry 2006.

48 Michael Cosgrove, "The Secret Story of the Jews Saved by Corsica in WWII," Digital Journal, October 27, 2010, www.digitaljournal.com/article/299465.

49 "CIA and FBI Used Thousands of ex-Nazi War Criminals as Spies and Concealed It from Congress and DOJ," Daily Kos, October 27, 2014, www.dailykos.com/story/2014/10/ 27/1339461/-CIA-and-FBI-used-thousands-of-ex-Nazi-war-criminals-as-spies-and-concealed-it-from-Congress-and-DOJ.

50 Robert Whiston, "Hitler's Gold – Part 1," January 2012, rwhiston.wordpress.com/2012/01/11/13/.

51 שרגא עילם "האיש שלנו בדמשק" "Our Man in Damascus," Haaretz, March 15, 2007.

52 Walter Rauff, Wikipedia, en.wikipedia.org/wiki/Walter_Rauff.

53 Simon Wiesenthal, "Mossad and MI6 Hired Nazi Walter Rauff," April 2, 2007, randompottins.blogspot.ca.

54 Jerry Meldon, "How Wall St. Bailed Out the Nazis," Consortium News, May 14, 2014, consortiumnews.com/2013/06/06/how-wall-st-bailed-out-the-nazis.

55 DPA, "West German Spy Agency Reportedly Hired Nazi War Criminal after WWII," Haaretz, September 26, 2011, www.haaretz.com/print-edition/news/west-german-spy-agency-reportedly-hired-nazi-war-criminal-after-wwii-1.386695.

56 take 903

57 http://rotter.net/forum/gil/5418.shtml#108.

58 Holocaust Learning, Nazi Persecution of the Jews: A Timeline, holocaustlearning.org/uploads/resources/ timeline%20of%20persecution.pdf.

59 Museum of Tolerance, Online Multimedia Learning Center, "36 Questions About the Holocaust," motlc.wiesenthal.com/site/pp.asp?c=gvKVLcMVIuG&b=394663.

Index

A

African gold 21
Alexandria 70
Algeria 34, 117
Ali Baba 27
Argentina' 147

B

Belgium 31
Ben Ali 158
Benghazi 26
Bey 141
BIS 17
Bourguiba 102, 115

C

Chile 154
CIA 146, 148
Corsica 15, 16
Cross 153
Czechoslovakia 17

D

Daily Mail 59
Der Spiegel 131
Djerba 37
Doolittle 116

E

Egypt 23, 90
Eli Cohen 150
Emperor Haile Selassie I 57
Erwin Rommel 30
ERWIN ROMMEL 121
Ethiopia 21, 83

F

Fish Operation 17
Fleig 15
Freedman 134

G

Gaza 47
Gilles Bernheim 140
Golden Ark 66

H

Haile Selassie 84
Halifax, 16
Henry Samuel 53
Hirschberg 138
Hitler 98, 100, 101
Holocaust 82

I

India 25
Israel 56

J

Jan Bart Gewald 24
JRSO 33

K

Karin Albou 137
Kirner 59
Klarsfeld 156

L

Libya 25

M

Mordechai Emanuel Noah 22
Muammar Gadhafi 25

N

New York Times 25

O

Odyssey Marine 49
Operation Torch 87
Ottoman 23

P

PATTON 118
Peter Hanining 16
Poseidon 14

Q

Queen of Sheba 67

R

REPARATION 74
Robin Leigh 60
Rommel 10, 15, 99
Ruth Kimche 154

S

Shalheveth Freier 161
Shlomo Nakdimon 148
Shraga Elam 149
South Africa 20
Sudan 21
Swiss National Bank 73
Switzerland 44

T

Tel Aviv 75
Telegraph 54
The Bey 37
Timothy Mason 80
Tom Bower 74
Tripoli 28

W

Walther Rauff 58, 149
White Gold. 25
Wolfgang Lotz 149

Y

Yemen 56
Yosi Reuven 138

www.ingramcontent.com/pod-product-compliance
Lightning Source LLC
Chambersburg PA
CBHW071504040426
42444CB00008B/1481